ARCHESTRATUS
THE LIFE OF LUXURY

Frontispiece. A fragment of a South Italian vase illustrating a grotesque character from comedy, dating to around 350 BC and found in Gela.

ARCHESTRATUS

FRAGMENTS FROM
THE LIFE OF LUXURY

A MODERN ENGLISH TRANSLATION
WITH INTRODUCTION AND COMMENTARY

JOHN WILKINS & SHAUN HILL

REVISED EDITION

ILLUSTRATIONS BY
PHILIPPA STOCKLEY

PROSPECT BOOKS
2011

Published in 2011 by Prospect Books,
Allaleigh House, Blackawton, Totnes, Devon TQ9 7DL.

The first edition of this book was published by Prospect Books in 1994.

BRITISH LIBRARY CATALOGUING IN PUBLICATION DATA:
A catalogue entry for this book is available from the British Library.

ISBN 978-1-903018-62-0

Typeset by Lemuel Dix and Tom Jaine.

Printed and bound in Malta by Gutenberg Press Ltd.

CONTENTS

Figure 1. A banqueting scene illustrating furniture, entertainment and hetairai, *the female 'companions' of non-citizen status who were the only women at the banquet/ symposium. The painting is on a bowl for mixing wine and water at a feast (* krater *), and is dated to the late fourth century* BC.

ACKNOWLEDGEMENTS
TO THE FIRST EDITION

We are most grateful for advice on several matters from Susanna Braund, W. Geoffrey Arnott and Tom Jaine. Particular thanks go to Alan Davidson for castigating a number of errors. Naturally, we are responsible for the text as published.

JOHN WILKINS AND SHAUN HILL, 1994

A NOTE ON THE ILLUSTRATIONS
AND THE COVER

The illustrations fall into two categories. The first group is taken from the Greek cities of southern Italy in approximately the period of Archestratus. Their purpose is to give some idea of the ways in which this rich culture represented its attitudes to eating in artifacts and artistic forms.

The second group represents some of the cities mentioned by Archestratus in his poem. In some cases these overlap with the first group, since he includes a number of Italian towns in his survey.

The artist Philippa Stockley has drawn her own interpretations of pottery vase-paintings and fragments. They purport to be accurate renderings, yet are not in any sense measured drawings or replicas.

The cover shows the design from a sixth-century Spartan cup exported to Tarentum. The workmanship and subject matter belie the austere image of Sparta in later centuries. Tarentum, a city of good living and good eating, was a Spartan colony (traditional date of foundation, 706 BC).

ALPHABETIC AND NUMERIC KEYS TO THE MAPS OF PLACES
MENTIONED BY ARCHESTRATUS

Abdera, 30
Abydus, 42
Aegina, 16
Aenus, 33
Ambracia, 10
Anthedon, 18
Athens, 15
Bolbe, Lake, 29
Bosporus, 35
Byblos, 60
Byzantium, 34
Calydon, 11
Caria, 55
Carystus, 21
Cephalodium, 6
Chalcedon, 40
Chalcis, 19
Copais, Lake, 23
Crete, 58
Delos, 47
Dium, 25
Eleusis, 13
Ephesus, 50
Eresos, 45
Eretria, 20
Erytbrae, 48
Gela, 1
Hipponium, 8
Iasus, 54
Lesbos, 43
Lipari, 9
Lydia, 57
Maeotic Lake, 37
Maroneia, 32
Megara, 24
Messina, 3
Miletus, 52
Mytilene, 44
Olynthus, 27
Parium, 41
Pella, 26

Pelorum, 4
Phaleron, 14
Phoenicia, 59
Pontus, 36
Rhegium, 7
Rhodes, 56
Samos, 51
Sicyon, 12
Sinope, 38
Strymon, River, 39
Syracuse, 2
Tegea, 17
Teichioussa, 53
Tenos, 46
Teos, 49
Thasos, 31
Thebes, 22
Torone, 28
Tyndaris, 5

1, Gela
2, Syracuse
3, Messina
4, Pelorum
5, Tyndaris
6, Cephalodium
7, Rhegium
8, Hipponium
9, Lipari
10, Ambracia
11, Calydon
12, Sicyon
13, Eleusis
14, Phaleron
15, Athens
16, Aegina
17, Tegea
18, Anthedon
19, Chalcis
20, Eretria
21, Carystus

22, Thebes
23, Copais, Lake
24, Megara
25, Dium
26, Pella
27, Olynthus
28, Torone
29, Bolbe, Lake
30, Abdera
31, Thasos
32, Maroneia
33, Aenus
34, Byzantium
35, Bosporus
36, Pontus
37, Maeotic Lake
38, Sinope
39, Strymon, River
40, Chalcedon
41, Parium
42, Abydus
43, Lesbos
44, Mytilene
45, Eresos
46, Tenos
47, Delos
48, Erythrae
49, Teos
50, Ephesus
51, Samos
52, Miletus
53, Teichioussa
54, Iasus
55, Caria
56, Rhodes
57, Lydia
58, Crete
59, Phoenicia
60, Byblos

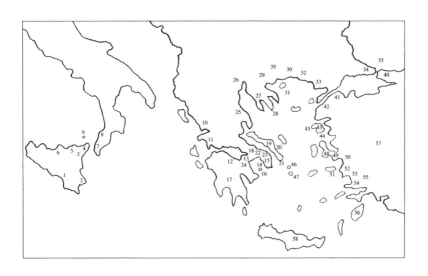

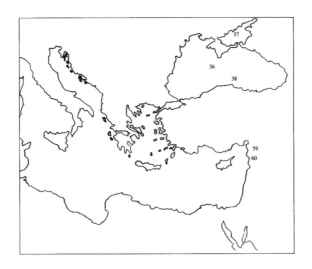

Figure 2. Apulian krater *(mixing bowl for wine) portraying men in a comedy carrying bread or meat on a spit. Athenaeus leads us to believe they are carrying bread in a religious procession. The vase is dated to 380–350 BC.*

INTRODUCTION TO THE FIRST EDITION

THE LIFE OF LUXURY

The Life of Luxury is a remarkable and almost unique work. When considering the ancient Greeks, the modern person may think of their temples, their tragedies, their philosophy and democracy. These best-known aspects of Greek culture are often specifically Athenian rather than Greek in general. Cookery books in ancient Greece do not readily come to mind; cookery in fact is credited by modern people – wrongly – to the Romans with their dormice and the cookery book ascribed to Apicius. Here we redress the balance by editing a Greek cookery book, not from Athens but from Gela in Sicily.

The Life of Luxury reveals much about Greek culture, and a great deal about the style of Greek food in antiquity. In travelling throughout the Greek world – Greece, southern Italy and Sicily, the coast of Asia Minor, the Black Sea – Archestratus makes clear how cosmopolitan Greeks were (rather like the British during the period of Empire). His influences – ingredients, combinations of flavours, techniques – are drawn from a wide Mediterranean background, taking in a diversity of ideas unrestricted by the topography of the Greek mainland.

Our commentary is concerned principally with the *content* of the poem, that is, the purchase and preparation of certain foods. Literary and other aspects of the poem have been investigated by Brandt (1888) and Degani (1990), and are considered by us only briefly.

Almost nothing is known about Archestratus other than that he was a Sicilian Greek, from Syracuse or Gela. The poem is conventionally dated to about 330 BC, partly in relation to the Pythagorean philosopher Diodorus of Aspendus mentioned in fragment 23, but whose dates are no more secure than Archestratus'. Archestratus was known to Clearchus the philosopher (*c.* 340–*c.* 250 BC) and therefore cannot post-date his death.

The Life of Luxury was valued by Athenaeus in his *Philosophers at Dinner* (in Greek *Deipnosophistai*), which was composed in about AD 200. He is the only ancient author to preserve the 62 fragments of the poem, which says much. By contrast, lost works of ancient poetry are usually preserved in quotations by a number of authors – for instance the multiple references drawn from the one hundred or more lost tragedies of Sophocles. This almost unique source for the poem may reflect the fact that Archestratus appears to employ little colourful or unusual vocabulary in the fragments: rare words are generally picked up by glossaries and grammarians. More likely, though, the lack of interest demonstrates the status of food books and recipe books: they are not high literature and are not carefully preserved in manuscripts for posterity. We would like to see the book on breadmaking by Chrysippus of Tyana or the book on salt fish by Euthydemus of Athens, but they survive only in sparse references in Athenaeus. In Wilkins and Hill (1994b) we discuss Mithaicos, an influential Syracusan predecessor of Archestratus, who survives only in four tiny fragments.

An exception to the general neglect of classical texts on cookery is *de arte coquinaria* of Apicius. This contains little of Apicius himself, being largely a compilation of recipes from different sources, but at least something has been preserved, and was thought worthy of preservation. There were many medieval copies made, and it was a scholarly favourite of the Renaissance.

It is evidently a risky business to attempt a reconstruction of the whole of Archestratus' poem from a mere 62 fragments, and we do not attempt to guess more than to hazard it unlikely there was much if anything on the cooking of meat, and that the bulk of the poem was devoted to fish [Wilkins (1993a)]. There may have been something on desserts, since there clearly is something on simple hors d' oeuvre, and while Athenaeus has much to say on sweet pastries and desserts, it is impossible to discern if he ignored Archestratus or the sage was indeed dumb. The section on breads may have been more extensive; we may have been told which breads were particularly suitable for which foods. The section on garlands and the organization of the feast [fragments 59–62] may have been much larger, though we might guess that such detail would have given Athenaeus more ammunition with which to attack the supposed luxury of Archestratus and would be likely to be quoted. We would certainly expect detail on sauces to be quoted in Athenaeus, and on authorial vanity, since these would have been grist to Athenaeus' mill. Their absence in Athenaeus implies their absence from the poem.

One later writer who had read Archestratus was the Roman poet Quintus Ennius, author of tragedies and the *Annals*, an historical poem in epic metre.

Ennius was a southern Italian who was born in 239 BC and learnt both Latin and Greek. For Romans of later centuries his work represented some of the finest poetry in early Latin, in a grand, rough style. One surviving fragment is a Latin adaptation of Archestratus fragment 56. Ennius probably learnt Greek at Tarentum in southern Italy, indication that there at least, or somewhere very similar, *The Life of Luxury* was being read around the end of the third century BC and was made available to the Romans who at this period were heavily influenced by the Greek cities to the south.

A striking feature of *The Life of Luxury* is that it is written in verse. At the time of composition (fourth century BC), prose-writing had been known in the Greek world for over a century. Archestratus had the option to write in prose, as technical and scientific and philosophical writers in the sixth and early fifth centuries had not. This raises questions about his audience and the purpose of the poem. It was almost certainly not a hands-on cookery book but a volume to be enjoyed at a rich man's banquet and symposium.

People rarely read in private in the Greek world: rather, they – if they were the upper-class people regularly associated with literature in antiquity – *heard* literature recited to them at banquets, in particular at the drinking session (symposium) after the meal. This was an occasion for men: they were apart from their wives and enjoyed the ministrations of women of low status, as well as literature, while other entertainments might include dancers or drunken games [Athenaeus, Book 15; Lissarrague (1990); fragment 3]. Such literature might be lyrical poems, songs, recited epic or drama or history, or sub-literary forms based on dance and mime.

Archestratus' poem, then, is *literature*. The category of literature it falls into is parody, poetry with inappropriate characters or subject-matter. It is a parody of epic, the poetry of Homer and Hesiod about heroes and gods in hexameter verse. So one day at the symposium the entertainment might be a recitation of Hesiod's *Theogony*, the story of the family history of the Olympian gods; the next day it might be the poem of Archestratus. He provides a pleasing contrast, and urbanely focuses on the very activity that the audience was enjoying. As they bit into their olive relishes, or took a mouthful of tuna, the hexameters celebrated the best kind of tuna that could be found and the best way in which it could be prepared.

There was a long tradition of the genre of parody before Archestratus, on topics such as the celebrated *Battle of the Frogs and the Mice*, but often in the area of food and its consumption. We have a fragment from the *Parodies* of the sixth/fifth-century poet Xenophanes in hexameters on the subject of eating chickpeas at the symposium [Xenophanes fragment 18]; Hegemon of Thasos, a notable parodist of the late fifth century, and, Athenaeus tells us [407a], the poet who consoled the Athenians when they lost their army in Sicily in 413, identifies himself in one of his hexameter poems as 'foul Lentil Soup'; at roughly the same date as Archestratus, Matro wrote his *Attic Banquet*, in whose hexameters an elaborate meal is described in an accomplished and comic way. [On the literature of parody in which inappropriate foods are blended with Homeric hexameters, and on Matro in particular see Degani (1990, 1991, 1994).]

A flavour of Matro may be given by the following extract [Lloyd-Jones and Parsons (1983) 534.33–43 = Athenaeus 135c–d. Here and elsewhere the text of Athenaeus is referred to in the standard form of page number (of the Greek text) and subdivision a–f]:

> The daughter of Nereus also came, Thetis of the silver feet,
> The cuttlefish of the fair tresses, the dread goddess who speaks,
> The only fish to distinguish white from black.
> I saw too Tityus, glorious conger of the marshy lake,
> Lying in the cooking pots: he lay over nine tables in length.
> In his footsteps came the fish goddess with the white arms,
> The eel, who boasted that she had been loved in the embrace of Zeus,
> From Lake Copais, the home of the whole tribe of wild eels.
> Enormous was she, and two men who competed in the games,
> Such as Astyanax and Antenor, would not have been able
> To lift her with ease from the ground on to a cart.

Degani discusses such phrases as 'goddess with the white arms' and argues that they are not mere travesties of Homer [we discuss the sexuality of the eel in the note on fragment 8].

Parody, Athenaeus tells us [699b], was particularly enjoyed in Sicily, birthplace of Archestratus and home of the cookery book. But *The Life of Luxury* is quite unlike all the others in the collection of parodic poetry edited by Brandt in 1888. It is a poem which may have amusing touches but is first and foremost a work of instruction for the acquisition and preparation of good food. Although other interpretations, discussed by Degani (1994) and Gowers (1993), are possible and potentially valuable, we do not consider them here, beyond noting that

Gowers, writing on food in Roman literature, has shown how it is often a metaphor for a style of poetry. A light, elegant style of cooking, such as that promoted by Archestratus, could represent a similar style of poetry, which was indeed a prevailing style after 300 BC. Thus short witty poems were preferred to verbose epic, as sensitive seasoning might be preferred to pungent sauces.

We conclude with two further stylistic considerations. Many of the fragments concern fish, which, as Athenaeus observes at the beginning of his work, are virtually absent from Homer. This may be due to the selection made by Athenaeus, but is probably not, and is a subtle way in which Archestratus can please his audience by taking over the Homeric verse-form and filling it with decidedly un-Homeric fish. Equally, if we compare Archestratus with Hesiod, as Athenaeus does [fragment 23], we can see a pleasing contrast between Hesiod's insistence on the grinding hard work of the peasant in his *Works and Days* and Archestratus' advice for good and elegant living.

The second point is that Archestratus might have been more credible if he had written in prose. Why this flirting with parody? Flirtation is the right word, for the quantity of Homeric and Hesiodic phraseology is small compared with Matro or Hegemon. A prose work may have convinced us that this was a book for chefs, not a pleasing poem for their dilettante employers. Equally, it would probably have condemned the work to oblivion, for it was the versification and playfulness that caught the eye of Athenaeus and seduced him into quoting 62 fragments. Contrast the fate of Mithaicos who, though influential enough to outrage Plato, wrote in prose and is scarcely mentioned by Athenaeus.

The content is clearly influenced by the form and tone of the medium. Yet, despite the fact that this is epic parody, the advice about the selection, purchase and preparation of food is first rate. The man has much to say, and much of value to say. Since chefs were of low status and unlikely to be sufficiently educated to write an epic-style poem, we presume that Archestratus was not a chef himself; but he has knowledge of quality produce and combinations of flavours and use of heat in cooking. He is perhaps an equivalent of an Edwardian lady, the kind of lady who supervised her kitchen and was concerned to try new dishes she had read about, but who was quite distinct from her cook below stairs.

The cook in antiquity was of low status, but the best chefs operated in a competitive mode, being hired out together with their brigade of assistants to the homes of the rich. Quality and fame mattered to them. The evidence for this is to be found in Greek comedy and therefore has to be treated with some caution, but we have argued elsewhere [Wilkins & Hill (1993)] that the comic chef bears a close relation to his counterpart in everyday life.

Writing about food in a practical way in ancient Greece was first and foremost a sub-division of medical writing. Food influenced the balance of the humours in the body. But eating is also a sensual experience: however basic the diet, senses of taste and smell and sight are necessarily involved. There is a hint of pleasure, directing writing on food towards the playful area of comedy. There are comic touches in Archestratus [fragments 9, 23, 35, 45], and there is some similarity between some of his advice and that found in speeches delivered by chefs in comedy.

The comic poets thought it desirable to have a comic chef as a stock character in their plays. The comic chef has to be recognizable in his comic guise, a caricature of his counterpart in the real world. As well as cooking methods, there are extravagant claims to reading, knowledge and excellence in the competitive world of the commercial chef. We offer two extracts.

A: Sophon of Acarnania and Damoxenus of Rhodes were fellow pupils of each other in the chef's art, and Labdacus of Sicily was their teacher. These two wiped away the clichéd old seasonings from the cook books and did away with the mortar: no cumin, vinegar, silphium, cheese, coriander – seasonings which old Kronos used to have. They did away with all these and said the man who used them was only a tradesman. All they asked for, boss, were oil and a new pot and a fire that was hot and not blown too often. With such an arrangement every meal is straightforward. They were the first to do away with tears and sneezing and a running nose at the table: they cleared out the tubes of the eaters. Well, the Rhodian died from drinking a salt pickle, for such a drink was unnatural.
B: Quite so.
A: Sophon now runs things in Ionia, and has become my teacher, boss. I myself philosophize, and I'm keen to leave behind me new books on the art of cooking.
B: O God! It's me you'll be butchering, not the animal you're about to sacrifice.
A: First thing in the morning you'll see me, books in hand, researching into food ways, in no way different from Diodorus of Aspendus.
Anaxippus, *Behind the Veil*, fragment 1.1–26KA
[Athenaeus 403e–f: this is Athenian comedy of the fourth/third century BC]

Anyone can prepare dishes, carve, boil up sauces and blow on the fire, even a mere commis. But the chef is something else. To understand the place, the season, the man giving the meal, the guest, when and what fish to buy, that is not a job for just anyone. You will get the same kind of thing just about all the time, but you will not get the same perfection in the dishes or the same flavour. Archestratus has written his book and is held in esteem by some, as if he has said something useful. But he is ignorant of most things and tells us nothing.

Dionysius, *The Law Maker*, fragment 2.15–26KA
[Athenaeus 405a–b: this is Athenian comedy of the fourth century BC]

In these comic passages we have a rejection of earlier techniques, consideration of location and season, an air of authority, all redolent of Archestratus. The first passage refers to Diodorus of Aspendus [see fragment 23]; Sophon of Acarnania is an influential chef mentioned elsewhere in Athenaeus; Archestratus himself appears in the second passage. These comedies and *The Life of Luxury* appear to draw on the same world of food preparation and writing about cooking.

These comedies, like *The Life of Luxury*, derive from the chefs of the Greek world in the fourth century. Comedy in Greek culture is an appropriate place for food and cooking to be commented on, perhaps because aspects of the real chef's life verge on the comic: complex and menial skills are combined in cooking; there is a sharp contrast between the heat of the kitchen and the calm of the banquet where the food is presented; there is an element of entertainment in the presentation of food, which might be mocked. Another parallel may be drawn between cooking and war: the kitchen is organized like a military operation, and indeed some military terminology is used. Then too, food has something in common with sex in being the object of pleasure [fragment 3].

THE GREEKS AT TABLE

Upper-class Greeks ate while they reclined on couches, putting food to their lips with one hand and leaning on the other arm. This has implications for the style of food. If it was eaten one-handed, then it needed to be presented on the plate in bite-sized portions. Even if it was a fish head [cf. fragments 18 and 20], it should be prepared for one-handed consumption. Knives were available, though almost certainly not spoons and certainly not forks. If the reclining posture were to be maintained, the easiest tool to supplement the human hand was bread; and if the bread was to act as a kind of scoop, then a flat bread like modern pitta appears eminently suitable, while a raised bread might be better for absorbing soups. We do not hear a great deal about raised breads in Athens at this period (we do at least hear about them, though), and the need for pitta-style scoops may account for Archestratus' praise of barley, discussed in the note on fragment 4. (He may of course be speaking in ignorance or in jest, but that is not our interpretation.)

They ate two sets of courses, all the while reclining on couches. In the first set, identified as the dinner (*deipnon*), appetizers with strong flavours [fragments 6–7] were followed by dishes based on fish and meat [fragments 8–58]. These dishes might be served several at a time. The second set of dishes accompanied the drinking session (symposium) [fragment 62]. This order of foods may be seen in Matro's *Attic Banquet* [quoted by Athenaeus 134d–137 c], and is adopted for the fragments of Archestratus, down to the provision of breads for the meal at the outset.

Courses were based on a carbohydrate element (*sitos*) – stomach-filling barley and wheat – with strong flavours (*opsa*) to provide extra proteins and vitamins and interest for the palate. These *opsa* ranged from best sea bass to a salad of bitter herbs or cheese and onions. Greedy people might eat too much carbohydrate, luxurious people too many *opsa*, particularly highly prized fish. After the food, the diners went into the drinking session (symposium) and were entertained.

The fragments, as we have seen, concentrate on fish-cooking (49 out of 62 fragments). It is our belief that fish was more highly valued by chefs than meat because meat was closely connected with other rituals, rituals of worship and sacrifice. The slaughter of animals in sacrifice and the butchering of the meat was the task of the *mageiros* (the Greek word for chef, butcher and sacrificer of animals): he divided the meat between the worshippers. It was possible to incorporate such worship with a banquet, but meat cookery appears only occasionally in cookery books. In Archestratus meat is represented only by hare (not a sacrificial animal) [fragment 57], goose [fragment 58] and sow's womb as a relish [fragment 62]. There may well have been more meat in the full poem and Athenaeus may have distorted the picture by his own lack of interest in meat; Greek culture nevertheless associated fish-eating (quality fish as opposed to small fry) with luxury and meat-eating with the gods. The full poem of Matro confirms the bias towards fish. This is in striking contrast with Christian Europe where fish is reserved for fast (that is, non-meat) days.

Archestratus cooks the fish simply, boiling, roasting or grilling, with light seasoning and oil added if it is quality fish, stronger flavours if poor quality [see fragments 13, 3, 45, 49]. Freshness and quality are his watchwords, and these features must not be damaged by strong sauces based on cheese and pungent herbs [fragment 45]. An earlier (or possibly alternative) style of cooking is deprecated [fragment 45] and a light, elegant style recommended. There is much interest in texture, both in parts of the fish, for instance head meat [fragments 18, 20, 22, 26, 33], fin [fragment 22], tail [fragments 26, 37, 40], and belly [fragment 23] as well as in varieties of fish.

Archestratus' favourite fish tend to have firm-textured and strongly flavoured meat rather than mild-tasting flesh like the white fish which are now used in France and Britain as the vehicles for sauces. And of course, he shows much interest in eels, the common eel, the conger and the moray [fragments 8, 16, 19]. He emphasizes flavour and the oil/fat of the fish where flavour is to be found [fragments 8, 12, 17, 18, 19, 30, 36, 45, 49]. Archestratus' presentation of fish has something in common with the Chinese approach as described in the modern manual of Yan-kit So. Comparisons with Far Eastern or South-East Asian cuisine are as appropriate as anything in modern Europe. An holistic approach to meal-time with emphasis on balance – yin and yang in China, humours in Greece – is common to both. The four humours, blood, phlegm, black and yellow bile, were to be kept in the right proportion and quality (hot, cold, wet and dry) by eating foods that would provide that balance and the required qualities.

Sauces of cheese or herb pickles are added to inferior fish, but in general this is not sauce-based cooking, the preference being for additions of oil and light herbs to the fish juices. This is striking, and to be contrasted with the strong flavours added to Roman foods (though our principal informant is 'Apicius' from the fourth century AD) and the meat-based sauces from Asia Minor which appeared in most other Greek cookery books: Athenaeus [516c–d] gives a list of books with one such recipe, and Archestratus' is notable for the absence of such sauces.

Meats are prepared with equal simplicity [fragments 57, 58] and an eye to essential juices. There is no interest (in the fragments at least) in comparatively new introductions to the Mediterranean such as pheasant and chicken.

Strong flavours are recommended at the beginning and end of the meal, in the form of olives, barley breads, small birds and pickled sow's womb. Vegetable dishes are deprecated in fragment 7 (whether as starters or in general is unclear). We do not have enough information on the presence of vegetables in the poem, but they may not have figured largely if associations with poverty, found elsewhere, were thought important by Archestratus. His views on chick peas and other desserts [fragment 62] lend some support to this suggestion, as does a dismissive remark at the end of fragment 23.

There is little more to say about the flavours in the poem for it relies principally on fresh produce, from the sea, which has changed less since antiquity than other products, certainly than farmed animals and plants. The product is cooked with little flavouring, and apart from the salt fish of fragment 38 and the occasional reference to silphium (the relative of the sulphurous asafoetida) there is little evidence of the predominate flavour we have found in ancient Greek food, that is a rank, slightly rotting quality. Often this is balanced with the sweetness of honey or olive oil to provide an equivalent harmony to more familiar couplings such as Stilton and sweet port wine or roast mutton and red currant jelly [Wilkins & Hill (1993)]. Anyone in the modern world who cooked from Archestratus would not find the flavours as strange as much ancient Greek food.

A comment on silphium is in order. It was the prestige flavour of antiquity. It was eaten more rarely than the strong Mediterranean herbs such as thyme, but was a much-desired flavour. It grew in North Africa in the area around Cyrene and there is little evidence for its growth elsewhere. The plant is one of the giant fennels which needed special conditions for its cultivation [Theophrastus *History of Plants* 6.3.1–7]. The root was eaten, but the main products were two juices, one derived from the root, the other from the stem. The export of silphium was an important part of Cyrene's trade in some periods. By the time of Nero the production was said by Pliny to be extinct, and the flavour thereafter was provided by asafoetida, another giant fennel, from Persia. Ancient sources on the enigmatic but pungent silphium have been discussed recently by Alice Arndt and Andrew Dalby in their papers listed in the bibliography.

ATHENAEUS AND ARCHESTRATUS

The attitude of Athenaeus himself is an interesting one, and for this reason we have quoted the *Context* of each citation as well as Archestratus' words themselves. Athenaeus' work, like Archestratus', is modelled on the banquet and symposium, and it explicitly introduces foods and rituals of the banquet as the diners progress through their meal [1b]. The ultimate literary model for a work of art based on the banquet and symposium is, Athenaeus tells us [2a], Plato (he means Plato's *Symposium*). Archestratus is mentioned by name early in the work, and his book is reported to have various titles [4e = fragment 1], implying that circulation was wide. Other food books are not given this prominence, though it must be said that the first two and a half books of Athenaeus have only survived in digest form and may have mentioned others in the longer original.

Archestratus appears among a mass of quotation from poets and philosophers, and before the account of the extraordinary diet of Homer's heroes, given near the beginning because the *Iliad* and *Odyssey* are considered the earliest record of eating in Greece and purveyors of meals consisting almost entirely of meat.

There is an important ambivalence in Athenaeus, a belief that in a sense Archestratus is worth quoting because he has something to say about food, but that at the same time something disreputable is creeping into the text from which Athenaeus must distance himself. Archestratus seems treated as authoritative at one moment, only to be disparaged later [fragments 2, 3, 38, 44].

Athenaeus is at times even hostile. He needs to use the poem for its detailed discussion of foods, particularly fish, but at the same time deprecates the luxurious associations the foods carry in Greek culture, especially in the philosophical tradition of the Stoics exemplified in fragment 3. A recurring criticism is Archestratus' excessive eye for detail, exemplified in fragment 2 or in the term *kimbix*, 'penny-pincher' or 'stickler for detail' in the introduction to fragment 37.

If we were to consider fresh produce for its own sake, there could be no objection to precision of location and species and preparation. The objection of course is not to the detail but to the 'luxurious' subject matter, which also, amusingly enough, is the subject matter of Athenaeus' own work.

A further objection is to the way Archestratus specified season by astronomical detail [fragment 3, and the note to fragment 26]. If we are only considering food, then the fish or plant may reasonably be eaten in its season [fragments 26, 36], when it is at its optimum. Aristotle for example shows how important season and location can be in fish [*History of Animals* 571a22–6]: 'in short, fish of the same species will not have the same season for impregnation, pregnancy, birth and general good condition in different places'. Location and condition of fish is what Archestratus considers, but an hostile observer may see this as an inappropriate and rather comic application of scientific detail to an unworthy area, the preparation of food. It may appear as over-fussy or over-credulous, as may the bio-dynamic approach to organic viticulture in the 1990s – to its critics. Some such idea lies behind the phrase 'Daedalus of tasty dishes' which describes Archestratus in the introductions to fragments 9, 22, 25, 35, 57, 62.

Athenaeus is not always negative. We said above that Archestratus was writing in the tradition of Hesiod [cf. fragment 23] but without the miserable peasant lifestyle portrayed by that poet. As in Hesiod, there is much knowledgeable detail; but by contrast, poverty is absent, as is a moralizing tone in the style of Theognis, another early poet with whom Archestratus is ironically compared in the introduction to fragment 23. Comparison with these poets makes clear what Archestratus' poem *is not*. But in the following passage [101f], it is debatable whether Athenaeus' tone is sincere or sardonic. 'We may well admire Archestratus, who gave us the excellent advice above [fragment 62]. He was a guide in pleasure for Epicurus the wise, and gives his advice memorably, like the poet from Ascra [Hesiod], and tells us not to listen to some, but to attend to him himself, and tells us to eat this and this, leaving out nothing that the cook has in Damoxenus the comic poet'. The passage is sardonic when judged in the *Context* of the places where Archestratus is criticized for offering pleasure [fragments 2, 3, 16].

Pleasure is the key. Archestratus' poem is after all called *The Life of Luxury* [fragment 1], and the sensual areas of luxury and pleasure had for centuries before Athenaeus been condemned by most philosophical systems as indicators of the uncontrolled and non-philosophical mind. Athenaeus dwells at length on this subject at 510a to 554f. When setting up the dietary system in his ideal state, Plato prescribes a simple vegetarian diet [*Republic* 372–3]; when it is objected that this is food fit for pigs, and that meat and couches to recline on are required, the response is, 'Ah! It seems we are not describing how to establish a city, but how to establish a luxurious city'. Dancing girls, sweet cakes and other 'luxuries' are then added, with grave fears for justice in the city. In his dialogue *Gorgias*, Plato sets up a structure of genuine and false skills with cooking as the lowest and most meretricious [463e5–466a3]. Ideas such as these pervade later thought, of which Athenaeus is an undistinguished example. Further examples can be seen in Macrobius, *Saturnalia* (fourth/fifth century AD), where in one passage Plato and Aristotle are quoted on the dangers of pleasure [2.8.7–15], and in another a doctor considers whether drinking or eating is the more pleasurable [7.12.20]. Medical texts are of course very different from philosophical texts on ethics. The body clearly does experience pleasure: it is a scientific and medical fact. Galen,

Figure 3. A Cyrenian trihemiobol portraying (on the reverse) three silphium plants, and on the obverse (not shown) the head of Cyrene, the local goddess (425–375 BC).

the most eminent of the ancient doctors, sometimes notes without comment a food as giving pleasure [see on fragment 13], while at others advises nutrition in preference to pleasure. (This latter attitude would have pleased Plato who in the *Gorgias* passage sees the doctor as prescribing the nasty medicines required and the cook offering sweet tastes which do no good.) [For an accessible analysis of Greek concepts of pleasure see Foucault (1985).] Archestratus alludes slyly to the moral debate about pleasure in fragments 23 and 31.

Archestratus, then, is a kind of figurehead, an Escoffier as it were, who, in Athenaeus' survey of Greek cooking, epitomizes and represents all aspects of it. If he has a certain austerity, then that can be used against him as easily as if he were a boaster or led a dissipated life. It is always possible of course that the world had moved on by the time of Athenaeus, and Archestratus was considered noteworthy but laughably old-fashioned.

ARCHESTRATUS AND THE GREEK WORLD

Archestratus comes from Gela. His provenance is significant. In the fifth and fourth centuries the Greek mainland was generally considered by its inhabitants to be agriculturally poor (Greece proper did not include the more fertile plains of Thrace or Macedonia); envious – and disapproving – eyes were cast to east and west, to the Greek cities on the Aegean coast of Turkey where there was influence from the oriental empires of Persians and others, and to the fertile lands of Sicily and southern Italy. In this rich western location with good land, wealthy monarchs in some cities, and a perceived higher standard of living, good cooking developed.

[23]

Gela is a good example of a city in a fertile plain which became influential in the century before Archestratus (though monarchical government proved a mixed blessing). The ingredients of sufficient produce, sufficient interest and sufficient wealth to allow choice combined to create an inventive experimentation with food, comparable perhaps with France in certain periods. Sicily is often referred to in poetry as an island of many fruits; Sybaris, Croton and Tarentum were cities of legendary luxury; local agriculture was fertile [Varro *On Agriculture* 1.4.4, Strabo *Geography* 6.1.12]. Epicharmus, the Syracusan comic poet of the early fifth century, had long lists of foods in some of his plays, fragments of which survive. In the best-preserved, *The Marriage of Hebe*, dozens of fish are listed. Aristophanes in the late fifth century identifies Sicily with good eating; we hear of Sicon (a Sicilian?), either a chef or foodwriter; Plato [*Epistle* 7] deplores Sicily as a gluttonous place where men eat two banquets a day and never sleep alone at night [for the moralizing combination of food and sex see fragment 3]. Plato cites the Sicilian Mithaicos as an early writer of a cookery book and Sicily as a place obsessed with food [*Gorgias* 518b]; at *Republic* 404d, Socrates speaks of 'those refinements of Sicilian cookery for which the tables of Syracuse are famous'. All this before Archestratus.

Later food writers associated with the area are: Heracleides of Syracuse (there are two writers with this name), Dionysius of Syracuse, Agis of Syracuse, Hegesippus of Tarentum. We cannot of course assume that because Archestratus came from Gela he lived there all his life [fragments 34 and 35].

It is very clear that much of the poem concerns not the cooking and the recipes but the selecting and purchase of the best produce that could be found. The imagined audience for the poem takes a gastronomic tour, like Egon Ronay or the editor of the *Good Food Guide*. In this situation, the gastronome does not stay at home and hire the best chef in town; rather, he – the intended recipients of this advice are almost certainly men – travels to whichever city offers the best of the desired produce, and there ensures that the produce is prepared in the correct way. Travel in the Greek world was widespread for certain groups of people. Traders above all led contacts between cities and with non-Greek peoples like the Phoenicians, Carthaginians and Egyptians. They were men of fairly low status, but of great importance, especially in the areas of foods such as wines, grains, and salted products like fish, and luxury goods [McKechnie (1989) 178–203]. Much of the poem concerns the buying of foods in markets, albeit in this case locally produced.

In the fourth century mercenaries also travelled widely [McKechnie (1989) 79–100]. Archestratus refers to mercenaries in fragment 61. A further category of traveller was the expert, the skilled worker, the doctor, the poet, the philosopher, the teacher of rhetoric [McKechnie (1989) 142–77]. Known travels of poets and philosophers such as Aeschylus and Plato imply much movement in the fifth and fourth centuries.

Archestratus' poem is clearly not influenced by Alexander the Great whose expeditions to the east introduced Asia and Asian products all the more strongly to the Greeks. Archestratus travels widely, but remains firmly in the Mediterranean and Black Sea with no exotic influences, except for the bakers of Phoenicia and Lydia [fragment 5] and the wine of Byblos [fragment 59], products which had been known to the Greeks for centuries.

Andrew Dalby (1994) would date the poem some 30 years earlier, in other words, to precede the destruction of Olynthus by Philip of Macedon, father of Alexander the Great, in 348 BC. How else can the reader be advised to buy a grey-fish at Olynthus [fragment 20]? Dalby may be right: the traditional date of 330 BC, referred to at the outset, certainly has little authority. It should be borne in mind, though, that Archestratus may have gathered his information over a long period: there is no necessary link between the date of a visit and the date of the composition of the poem. If this is the case then Archestratus appears as well-travelled, but not within a short space of a year or two. Dalby [1994, and in his thesis *Unequal Feasts. Food and its Social Context in early Greece* (Birkbeck College, London 1993), later published as Siren Feasts (1996)] has much useful comment on cities visited by Archestratus (to him we owe the Strabo quotation on fragment 30).

Dalby (1994) also describes the Mediterranean in the fourth century as a dangerous place, with Carthaginians marauding in Sicily and Italy, Dionysius of Syracuse meting out destruction in Italy, Persia threatening cities in Asia Minor such as Erythrae, the Macedonians taking over Greek cities in the Aegean. We find his dating convincing, his description of danger less so. There were upheavals, not least in the domination of the Macedonians and Alexander the Great in the Aegean area, but travel was still possible, as it always had been.

Gela itself was a dangerous place in the first half of the fourth century, as a focus of Syracusan and Carthaginian ambitions, but sailing from Italy to Greece and from city to city was what Greeks had always done, and what Archestratus recommends in nearly every fragment. He is not wistfully proposing an unrealistic itinerary: we should think of the cities mentioned as accessible.

The poem takes us to some out-of-the-way places. Ambracia [fragments 15, 25, 30, 56] in western Greece is striking (though note Sophon of Acarnania, a chef from a similar area quoted in a comic passage above), Anthedon in Boeotia [fragment 14] perhaps less so. This type of place is to be contrasted with a city like Byzantium which is traditionally associated with all kinds of fish, or Miletus which traditionally supplies good sea bass in Aristophanes and the comic tradition.

THIS EDITION

For our translation we have used the numeration of Brandt (1888) and the text of Lloyd-Jones and Parsons (1983) except where stated. The fragments are organized to follow the order of a Greek meal.

In the poem itself, as successive products are introduced, a number are named at the beginning of the verse, with or without the definite article [fragments 6, 8, 9, 11, 12, 14, 18, 30, 41, 43, 44, 47, 50, 52, 53, 54, 55, 56, 57], and another series is introduced with 'and X' at the beginning of the verse [14, 19, 27, 35, 37, 46, 48, 49]. This organization of the poem as if it were a catalogue or list of food products is notable, but not followed in all cases. In one case, the same fish appears to be mentioned twice [fragments 13 and 41]. A feature of a number of fragments is to give alternative, often local, names for a fish. This is particularly appropriate for fish which attract different names in different ports, and is a practice adopted by Alan Davidson in *Mediterranean Seafood*.

For fish we have used the ancient authors Oppian *On Fishing*, Aristotle *History of Animals*, Dorion and other authorities quoted in Athenaeus, and Galen *On the Qualities of Foods* to give a wide coverage of approaches, literary, zoological and medical. We have exercised some caution in the identification of species in Archestratus' poem, mindful of Alan Davidson's observation in his 'Note on Mediterranean Fish in Classical Times' [Davidson (1981) 225–7]: 'we find, with a pleasurable feeling of sympathy, as much confusion in the nomenclature of fish in the ancient world as there is nowadays'.

INTRODUCTION TO THE REVISED EDITION

There have been major developments in the study of our poet Archestratus since the first edition of Europe's earliest writer of a surviving cookery book appeared in 1994. These developments may be divided into three categories. The first is scholarship on Archestratus and his poetry. Secondly, innovative work has been published on the historian of ancient dining, Athenaeus of Naucratis, who preserved nearly all our fragments of Archestratus, and integrated him into the Roman world. Thirdly, there have been numerous publications on food in the ancient world in general, which enable us to place Archestratus more accurately in the history of dining. As a coda on this history, we will reiterate our understanding of the preferred taste profile of Greek and Roman food.

Before reviewing these publications, we summarize the key issues that have emerged.

Archestratus, writing in the fourth century BC, fits a pattern of luxurious eating that was transmitted from the court of Persia of the fifth century BC through the Greek-speaking Hellenistic courts of the successors of Alexander the Great to the imperial court of Augustus and his successors in Rome.
The poem of Archestratus remained a point of contention 600 years after its composition, for ethical as much as culinary reasons.
Athenaeus of Naucratis might be a much more sophisticated author than has sometimes been thought.
Ancient Greek food tasted distinctly different from modern 'Mediterranean' flavours; different, not worse.

A major edition of Archestratus was brought out in 2000 by two American scholars, S. Douglas Olson and Alexander Sens. They re-edited the Greek text of Archestratus preserved in the manuscripts of Athenaeus, provided translations into English and extensive notes on plants and animals, with, in addition, particular emphasis on the poetic vocabulary and rhythm, borrowed both from epic and other Greek poetry. In an introductory essay, they comment on structure and contents, audience and reception, and dialect, language and style. They bring out the poetic qualities of the poem (for which see also Wilkins 2000) and the likelihood that it was composed for recitation at elegant symposia. Their judgement is judicious and cautious, sharing, for example (p. xxii), our reservations (p. 31) on Andrew Dalby's attempt to date the poem to before the destruction of the Greek city of Olynthus in 348 BC, as mention of it later would be tasteless, in Dalby's view. Dalby's chapter on Archestratus appeared in Wilkins, Harvey & Dobson in 1995, and he added more in his *Siren Feasts*, which is mentioned below. Wilkins 2008, also mentioned below, tries to locate Archestratus (of the fourth century BC) in the world of Athenaeus (late second/early third century AD). Archestratus was very useful to Athenaeus as a repository of details about fish and places to eat it, but at the same time immoral, in Athenaeus' view, because in his poem, not to mention the very title of the poem, he was urging readers to indulge their pleasures. Archestratus appealed to the scholar in Athenaeus but horrified the moralist. As a writer on pleasure, Archestratus was a man of his century, which contained the attacks of Plato on pleasure, the birth of Epicurus, the advocate of pleasure as a goal (within strict limits) and also the first use of the word *hedupatheia*, 'the experience of sweet things', which Archestratus used as his title and we have translated as *The Life of Luxury*.

A final area discussed by Olson and Sens remains to be mentioned. They re-order the fragments of Archestratus slightly, bringing fragment 56 forward to become their fragment 7, because 'shellfish are referred to a number of times specifically as appetizers' (p. 39). Athenaeus gives ample support to this claim in his third book, but we have not followed this suggestion for two reasons. First, Athenaeus (14.642e–f) mentions a passage from a comedy of the fourth century BC which includes one of the species in fragment 56, clams [Olson and Sens 2000, p. 42 identify *kongkai* in fragment 56 (their fragment 7) as 'clams'; we, more tentatively, declare them (p. 85) an unidentified shellfish], among the 'second tables' or dessert dishes, and Petronius in his *Satyricon* mentions oysters among the dessert dishes served at Trimalchio's feast. Petronius is writing about a city in the bay of Naples in about 70 AD, which brings us to our second point. Athenaeus, the Greek-speaking author setting his fictional meals in the Rome of about 200 AD, has Ulpian, his master of ceremonies, speak as follows (3.101b):

The ancients [unspecified] however, all of them, did not serve sow's wombs or lettuce or anything else of the kind before the main courses, as happens now. Archestratus at least, the Daedalus of cooking, speaks of sow's womb after the dinner and the toasts and the anointing with perfumes [fragment 62 follows].

Athenaeus quotes fragments 62 and 56 at the beginning of his work, and makes a point of identifying the order of the dishes as a matter of variation in the period between the time of Archestratus and his own. Since it is theoretically possible to serve shellfish at the dessert stage, we have not changed the traditional order of Brandt 1888.

We need to understand Athenaeus of Naucratis, the author who has almost single-handedly preserved Archestratus for posterity, because the part of Archestratus' poem that has survived is his selection and his choice may well have shaped our impression of the *Life of Luxury*. Athenaeus has enjoyed much scholarly attention in the last seventeen years. A major re-evaluation was published in 2000, with two more to follow in 2001 and 2008 [Braund and Wilkins 2000, Jacob 2001, Wilkins 2008].

Braund and Wilkins 2000 include a number of evaluations of Athenaeus as a transmitter of quotations by lost authors. Chapters by Pelling on general problems of separating fragments from their conversational context in the *Deipnosophists* and by Walbank on Polybius, the Greek historian of Rome's rise as a regional power, are particularly helpful for considering how Athenaeus has selected, used and adapted Archestratus. Useful too is Lenfant 2007, who has edited chapters on historians quoted by Athenaeus, a number of them dating from Archestratus' own period, the fourth century BC. Zecchini in this volume added further to his important observations in 1989 on authors quoted in Athenaeus.

From a different perspective, Wilkins 2007 argues that while Athenaeus used canonical authors such as Homer, Plato and Aristotle to orient perspectives among the Deipnosophists, he uses Archestratus to guide the reader through complex issues connected with food. This case is developed further in Wilkins 2008, where Archestratus is shown to be good on zoology, gastronomy and geography, but bad on pleasure and incitement to misconduct, and, most of all, to contribute to the pressures of wealth and extravagance that threaten the Deipnosophists' own world at their dinners with Larensis in the third century AD. This is why Athenaeus introduces fragment 21 of Archestratus (p. 57 below) with reference (a) to the famously luxurious Assyrian king Sardanapalus (for whom see p. 39) and (b) to the fish that Romans now carry into the dining room to the 'accompaniment of pipes and garlands'.

Athenaeus is trying to bring together the Greek past, as represented by Archestratus and hundreds of other writers on food and drink, and the Roman present. That is an important objective in the second and third centuries AD, and an important landmark for us in the reception of *The Life of Luxury.* However, Archestratus had also been translated into Latin centuries earlier, by Ennius the epic poet. His *Annals* were part of the stern tradition of the Roman Republic, but Ennius was also master of three languages, Latin, Greek and Oscan, and, like Archestratus, was a poet from the south of Italy, from the Messappii of the heel of Italy, near Tarentum. Eleven lines of his translation are preserved by Apuleius in his *Apology* (39.2), with the following introduction:

Quintus Ennius wrote a *Hedyphagetica* in verse. He lists innumerable kinds of fish which he has obviously got to know diligently. I remember a few verses and will recite them:

'Just as the sea *mustela* is better than all others at Clipea,
There are many mussels at Aenus and rough oysters at Abydus.
The scallop is at Mytilene and at Charadrus in Ambracia.
The sargue is good at Brundisium. Get it here, if it is big.
Note that the boar-fish is first rate at Tarentum.
Make sure you buy the *elops* at Surrentum, and the *glaukos* at Cumae.
Why have I omitted the parrotfish, the brain as it were of great Jove?
(It is big and good when caught near Nestor's home.)
And the *melanurus*, the *turdus* wrasse, the *merula* wrasse and the maigre?
At Corfu, octopus, the fat heads of the *acharna*,
The large and small purple shellfish, mussels, and also sweet sea-urchins.'

He adorned others in many verses and explains among which people each lives, and how each tastes best, roasted or cooked in its juices.

(There are many reminiscences of Archestratus' original here, not least fragment 56 in lines 2–3, and many of the fish species mentioned. Some of the place names however are new, such as Pylos (Nestor's home), Clipea (in North Africa), Sorrento and Brindisi. This seems to be a translation that is also adapting, possibly updating its material. Ennius lived 239–169 BC.)

Figure 4. Two diners on a vase of the second half of the fourth century are served cakes and fruits by a female servant; a young male servant attends to the wine cups.

The most striking contributions to a new approach to understanding Athenaeus are made in two essays by Christian Jacob (Jacob 2000 and Jacob 2001) in which he develops the idea of Athenaeus as a scholar and librarian, who organizes quotations in his vast work in the way that a librarian might refer to an ancient work, with care taken about genre, authorship, book number, and systems for cross reference. It was characteristic of the period to read the present by explicit reference to the past, a practice that can be seen in authors of the Roman imperial period who wrote in their native Greek language, such as Plutarch, Galen, Lucian, Porphyry and many others.

New translations of Athenaeus have appeared, in the Loeb series in the United States, and in Spain, Italy, Germany and Poland.

The third category of recent publications concerns the study of food in general in Greece and Rome. Studies based on anthropology have been influential in France, in particular Vernant and Detienne 1979 on cooking and sacrifice, and Detienne 1977 on food and cultural meaning. Demographic studies of the corn supply to ancient cities, especially Garnsey 1988, have been influential.

There has been work, too, on the institutions of the symposium and the shared meal (Murray 1990, Schmitt-Pantel 1992), and wide-ranging collections of essays on all aspects of eating (Longo and Scarpi 1989, Slater 1991, Murray and Tecusan 1995, and Wilkins, Harvey and Dobson 1995). Vössing 2004 published a major study of royal banquets. Numerous publications by Andrew Dalby have added much clarity and detail, while general overviews (Garnsey 1999 and Wilkins and Hill 2006) have brought out issues of nutrition and medicine, as had Grant 2000 and Powell 2003. Ecology and climate are the focus of Sallares 1991 and Hordern & Purcell 2000. Roller 2006 and Donahue 2005 have brought the largely Greek focus of these studies into the Roman sphere, in which, of course, Athenaeus sets the banquets of his Deipnosophists. Studies of the artistic images displayed in the dining room include Lissarrague 1990 (see our original bibliography) and Dunbabin 2003. The story of dining in the ancient world is completed by Grocock and Grainger's edition of Apicius, the compilation of cookery books from the fourth century AD, whose emphasis on heavy spicing anticipates medieval dining in Europe and the Arab world, as charted by Scully 1995 and Rodinson 2001.

Finally, the characteristic tastes of the food of Archestratus. When discussing taste on page 20 above, we refer to 'the predominate flavour we have found in ancient Greek food, that is a rank, slightly rotting quality'. Grocock and Grainger (2006) have taken exception to this statement, reading it as pejorative of Greek cooking. To clarify, we mean readers to understand by this simple description that Greek food did not normally taste like modern Mediterranean flavours, but was dominated by silphium or asafoetida, a sulphurous, garlicy flavour, more familiar to modern readers in India. Archestratus uses this sparingly, since much of his fish is cooked very simply.

FRAGMENTS FROM

THE LIFE OF LUXURY

Figure 5. One of a series of fish dishes from Cumae, near Naples, which are discussed by Trendall in Red-Figure Vases of Southern Italy and Sicily *(London, 1989), pages 169–70. The dishes are concave and hollow, with a hole at the centre of the upper surface into which juices from the fish may be collected, or sauce deposited. The series is further illustrated by figures 15 and 20, below. The fish at the bottom may be the striped bream, to the left, the two-banded bream.*

In the following pages, the words of Athenaeus are printed in italic (the *Context*), and his quotation from Archestratus (the content) is printed in Roman characters. Commentary on each fragment, divided between context and content, follows immediately.

FRAGMENT I
[ATHENAEUS 4E]

Archestratus of Syracuse or Gela [wrote] a work called by Chrysippus, 'Gastronomia', by Lynceus and Callimachus, 'The Life of Luxury', by Clearchus, 'An Account of Dining', by others 'The Art of Good Cooking', an epic poem whose first line is: I offer an exhibition of my investigations to the whole of Greece.

COMMENTARY

Context. Is Gela or Syracuse the home city? Since Syracuse was the more influential, especially in the world of food, Gela is more likely to be the correct city of origin. The sources are certain that he is Sicilian, the principal gourmet centre in the Greek world in the fourth century [see Introduction]. The poem is cited with various titles, suggesting either that it was well known or that it was often referred to, if by people who could not remember the title exactly. Lynceus (third century BC) was *a belle lettriste* who, according to Athenaeus, often referred to works on food; Callimachus (*c.* 310–240 BC) was the poet and librarian of the great library at Alexandria, whose evidence is generally believed. [On Chrysippus and Clearchus see fragment 3.] Further evidence in support of the title 'The Life of Luxury' (*hedupatheia*: lit. 'experience of sweet things') may be found in the adaptation by the Roman poet Ennius (born 239 BC). He follows Archestratus closely in the only fragment which survives (some 11 lines), and entitled his poem 'On Eating Sweet Things', *Heduphagetica*.

Content. The first line is a version in hexameter form of the opening words of Herodotus' *Histories*. This is important. Epic poems generally invoke the muses or gods to help and inspire the poet; Archestratus ignores such an invocation (unlike Matro) and presents his treatise, albeit with a flourish. Herodotus *publishes* his investigation; Archestratus *exhibits* his; but they are both investigations (*historiai*) of distant parts, dispassionately done. Archestratus has no narrow patriotism for his city, nor of course has Herodotus. It is notable, though, that Archestratus keeps within Greece, and does not follow Herodotus into Persia and the East [see Introduction]. He does however resemble Herodotus as a traveller before the great eastern stimulus provided by Alexander the Great. He is writing for 'the whole of Greece', that is in international terms the ancient world. Herodotus wrote his *Histories* some 100 years before Archestratus.

FRAGMENT 2
[ATHENAEUS 278D]

This Archestratus, in his love for pleasures, travelled over every land and sea with precision, in a desire, as it seems to me, to review with care the things of the belly; and imitating the writers of geographical descriptions and voyages, his desire is to set forth everything precisely, wherever the best to eat and the best to drink are to be found.

COMMENTARY

Context. Athenaeus describes Archestratus' motivations as pleasure and the belly (*gaster*): on pleasure see fragment 8; on a more forthright comment on the belly see the introduction to fragment 38; on reviewing with care and precision see fragment 37 and Introduction. Archestratus does indeed set forth detail carefully and impressively and is a model in his method which reviews various locations where the best of a product is to be found. Archestratus may be writing from hearsay or may have tested the products of these cities: exactly the same debate rages about Herodotus' descriptions of various locations. The writers of geographical descriptions and voyages are authors like Herodotus and his predecessors who wrote of distant cities and strange customs. Ultimately such works go back to the oral epics of Homer, with the voyages of Odysseus. [See further Pearson (1939) 1–108.] In the modern world many gastronomes pontificate from a platform which is no more than a variation on patriotism, the general purpose being a celebration of home produce and its use. Archestratus notes such people in fragment 60. Parallels can be drawn with current distaste for French apples in Britain despite the sometimes superior climate for apple growing in that country. It is difficult to imagine the popularity in Kent or Worcestershire of a book lauding Golden Delicious. Archestratus' voyages around the known world, to places not even controlled by Greeks, make his findings that much more valid [see Introduction].

Content. There is no certain content. Archestratus may or may not have made the declaration for the best quality food and drink.

FRAGMENT 3
[ATHENAEUS 457C]

In book one of his work on proverbs, Clearchus writes: 'the teasing out of riddles is not alien to philosophy, and the ancients displayed their educational training by means of them. In putting forward a riddle among the drinkers, they were not like modern people who ask, which form of sex is most pleasurable, or which or what kind of fish is sweetest, or which is most in season, or which is particularly eaten after Arcturus rises or the Pleiades or the Dog-star? In addition to this they offer as prizes for the winners kisses which are hateful to men of free birth and sensibility, and as punishment for the losers they stipulate the drinking of unmixed wine, which they drink more readily than the cup of health. In short, this is what you would expect of a man who was at home with the writings of Philaenis and Archestratus, and who was keen on the so-called Gastrologies ..'.

COMMENTARY

Context. Archestratus may have written something like, 'which fish and of what kind is the sweetest food, or which is most in season, which is eaten in particular either after Arcturus and the Pleiades or the Dog-star?' Athenaeus reports related opinions of philosophers at 335d–e. 'In book five of *On the Good and on Pleasure*, Chrysippus writes of "books of Philaenis and the 'Gastronomia' of Archestratus and stimulants for love and sex and in a similar way slave girls who become skilled in such movements and positions and practise for such things." Later he says: "they learn such things and acquire things written on such subjects by Philaenis and Archestratus and writers of similar works." In book seven he says: "just as the learning of the works of Philaenis and the 'Gastronomy' of Archestratus contribute nothing to the living of a better life." Now you who have quoted this Archestratus so many times have filled the symposium with unrestrained immorality, for which of the things that can damage us has that fine epic poet omitted? He is the only man who has emulated the life of Sardanapalus son of Anacyndaraxes.' At 337b, Athenaeus reports: 'Clearchus in his book on proverbs says that the teacher of Archestratus was Terpsion who was the first to write a Gastrology and to instruct his students in what foods they should avoid.' These fragments best state the hostile tradition which has in part infected Athenaeus [Introduction]. Clearchus (a Peripatetic philosopher in the school of Aristotle, 4th–3rd century BC) surveys various rituals of the banquet and articulates the ready association between eating and sex, linking at the same time Archestratus and the supposed authoress of a sex manual, Philaenis [on whom see Parker (1992)]. Clearchus wrote a *Book of Love* himself, and it is not entirely clear how it differed from Philaenis: in some way though Philaenis and Archestratus shared the unsatisfactory category of 'luxury'. Clearchus' scorn for fish in their season [on which see Introduction] makes it clear enough that Archestratus' poem is not for him.

Chrysippus the Stoic philosopher, who elsewhere [Athenaeus 101f and 104b] identifies Archestratus' poem with the whole of the philosophy of pleasure of Epicurus, attacks Archestratus and links him with Philaenis. Athenaeus' speaker adds a sarcastic note about the fine epic (parodic) poetry

Figure 6. A silver coin of Gela (c. 450 BC) portraying a river god and fish (fish were often part of the design on Sicilian coins).

of Archestratus, at this point introducing a further indication of immorality, the emulation of the life of Sardanapalus, king of Assyria in the sixth century BC [compare fragment 21]. This king was for the classical world the archetype of the luxurious oriental despot. Athenaeus reviews his 'excesses' at 528f–530c. There is almost nothing of the East in *The Life of Luxury*, and less than in most cookery books, but Archestratus stands as the figure-head for cooking in this hostile tradition [see Introduction]. On Greek ambivalence towards the East see Wilkins (1994). Nothing more is known of Terpsion.

FRAGMENT 4

[ATHENAEUS 111E]

Archestratus in his Gastronomy discourses on barley meal and breads as follows: First then I will list the gifts of Demeter of the fair tresses, my dear Moschus: keep it safe in your heart. Now the best to get hold of and the finest of all, cleanly bolted from barley with a good grain, is in Lesbos, in the wave-surrounded breast of famous Eresos. It is whiter than snow from the sky: if the gods eat barley groats then Hermes must come and buy it for them from there. In seven-gated Thebes too it is reasonably good, and in Thasos and some other cities, but it is like grape pips compared with Lesbian. Get that idea clearly into your head. Get hold of a Thessalian roll, rounded into a circle and well pounded by hand. They themselves call this roll *krimnitas*, but others call it *chondrinos* bread. Then I praise the son of fine wheat flour from Tegea, ash-bread. Bread made in the market, famous Athens provides for mortals, of an excellent quality. In Erythrae which bears clusters of grapes a white bread comes out of the oven, bursting with the delicate flavours of the season, and will bring pleasure at the feast.

COMMENTARY

Content. This long fragment is interesting mainly for showing the variety of bread making. Bread is more effectively and economically baked in quantity. The use of grains in porridge obviously better suits home preparation, especially as home ovens were primitive [Sparkes (1962)]. Competition in style and quality of bread would be stimulated by these market conditions: in this fragment commercial baking seems to be at the centre (Hermes god of markets, Athenian market bread); in the next, good home baking. Particular praise of fine barley flour is remarkable, but white barley is found

Figure 7. A bronze coin of the third century BC from Eresos on Lesbos. Head [Historia Numorum (Oxford 1911), p. 560] noted the close link between Archestratus' remarks on Hermes and barley and the coins of Eresos with a head of Hermes and an ear of grain. This is further evidence that the poem is firmly based in the markets and kitchens of the city states described.

elsewhere in fourth-century texts, such as the lyric poem, *The Banquet* of Philoxenus of Leucas and in the comedy of Alexis, *The Woman Drugged on Mandrake* [fragment 145]. Although he does not say so, Archestratus is probably describing flatbreads here, to which barley flour may give more flavour, while the gluten of wheats, necessary if using yeast, is not needed. The fragment is characteristic for its survey of quality products from certain cities, expressed with a hint of epic language. So 'Demeter of the fair tresses' and 'keep it safe in your heart' clearly derive from epic, while phrases such as '[ash bread] son of wheat flour' and flour 'whiter than snow' are characteristic of comedy and epic parody. 'The wave-surrounded breast of famous Eresos' has an epic ring but no clear epic antecedent. There is a notable reference to the gods favouring the barley groats of Eresos, clearly a mark of quality, similar to remarks in fragments 23 and 59–60. The way gods ate – for the Greek gods ate like all other creatures – took two forms. In the first they ate immortal foods – ambrosia and nectar and the smoke of marrow in thigh bones on sacrificial fires. In the second they shared human food, receiving a portion on an altar of first fruits or barley cakes before the humans ate. This was hospitality for a visiting god. That is what we have here, though there is something playful and exaggerated about this statement, helped by reference to Hermes god of exchange and commerce who in comedy is not beyond a little thieving and deception [Aristophanes, *Peace*]. The wheat bread of

Athens, praised here, was widely praised in Athenian sources also. Athens, an international centre, was able to import wheat on a scale many Greek cities could not match. Athenians exploited the opportunity by developing a famous range of breads and pastries. Moschus, one of the addressees of the poem [compare fragment 17]' is an equivalent of Perses, the addressee of Archestratus' model, Hesiod's *Works and Days. Krimnitas* and *chondrinos* derive from terms for coarsely milled barley.

Figure 8. A Boeotian terracotta of a woman kneading bread (early fifth century BC). *A number of similar activities – grilling, grating, roasting, putting rolls in an oven – were represented by Boeotian artists in this style. See Sparkes (1962). The chief town of Boeotia was Thebes.*

FRAGMENT 5
[ATHENAEUS FRAGMENT 112B]

After this [i.e. fragment 4] the chef Archestratus advises that you have a breadmaker from Phoenicia or Lydia, unaware of the fact that breadmakers from Cappadocia are the best: Get yourself a man from Phoenicia or Lydia in your house, a man who will know how to make every kind of bread product on a daily basis, whatever you order.

COMMENTARY

Context. Athenaeus' comments on the superiority of Cappadocian bread are irrelevant except to show continuing variety in bread-making. The term for chef (*tenthes*) also means gourmand and may be insulting.

Content. The advice to get a specialist foreign baker (a slave perhaps) into the house is clearly for the rich only. Bread provides breadcrumbs when dry, and is more portable than porridge (unless porridge is dried into bricks). Phoenician-style bread is more likely to be leavened, as is attested by biblical references to yeast. Greek sources speak of leavened bread, but much more commonly of flatbreads.

FRAGMENT 6
[ATHENAEUS 64A]

Archestratus: Bulbs. I bid farewell to vinegar-dishes of bulbs and plant stalks, and to all the other side-dishes.

COMMENTARY

Content. Bulbs, probably of the hyacinth and iris family, were often eaten as appetizers in antiquity, for example with a vinegar dressing. Their use in modern cooking in the Mediterranean world is described by Patience Gray [(1986) 53, 182, 190, 202]. She stresses their bitterness, a characteristic of many ancient plants, confirmed for asparagus bulbs by Galen [6.652–4 Kühn]. The mention of 'plant stalks' (*kauloi*) does not make clear what the stalks are. Cabbage is possible, the herb silphium the most likely. Silphium [see Introduction] is mentioned in Eubulus (quoted below) in association with bulbs, though it is odd that an expensive item is dismissed along with a cheap one (though see fragment 49 on silphium in a cheap dish – perhaps locally grown silphium was available at a much lower price). Athenaeus says [133a], 'the ancients used foods to whet the appetite, such as olives in brine': these are often referred to, and Archestratus' dismissal of all other side dishes as well is surprising. He could be dismissing all appetizers or a particular style of serving, or particular vessels, since olives are served in fragment 7; or he could be dismissing tired old appetizers in favour of simple but good quality matured olives. The language is similar to Eubulus fragment 7.3–5 (comedy of the mid-fourth century): 'I haven't come here to scoff plant stalks or silphium juice or sacrilegious and bitter side-dishes or bulbs'. Eubulus is Athenian: comedy is a further influence on Archestratus to place beside Homer and Hesiod. The majority of comedy was Athenian, but not all. The Sicilian poet Epicharmus has much on foods in his plays.

FRAGMENT 7
[ATHENAEUS 56C]

Archestratus in his Gastronomy: Let them serve you wrinkled and tree-ripened olives.

COMMENTARY

Content. In the passage quoting this fragment, Athenaeus lists many kinds of preparation for olives.

FRAGMENT 8
[ATHENAEUS 298E]

Concerning the eel Archestratus records this: Eels. I praise all eels, but by far the best is the eel caught from the sea off the straits of Rhegium. There, citizen of Messina, in being able to put such food to your lips, you are richer than all other mortals. Of course, the eels of Copais and Strymon have a great reputation for excellence. They're huge and amazingly fat. All in all I believe the eel lords it over everything else at the feast and is a guide to pleasure, though it is the only fish that has no scrotum.

COMMENTARY

Content. The eel (*egchelus*) is rich in oil and is now mainly used smoked or jellied in the UK. Eels are prized – especially the head – in Cantonese cooking

[Yan-kit So (1992) 267, 269]. The comparison with China is important since texture clearly counts for something in this poem, as seen in the use of head and tail meat [Introduction]. It may be the fat of the eels that made them attractive to the Greeks: this is comprehensible since they valued the flavour residing in the fat of fish in general, and the fattiness of the eel perhaps signified its pre-eminence over others. In this fragment, Archestratus covers sea, river and lake eels. The last are a puzzle, for Lake Copais (north of Thebes in Boeotia) has no access to the sea, except possibly by deep underground gullies, and the overland route to the sea appears too far and too hilly for eels to contemplate. A. Mair in his edition of Oppian [Cambridge, Mass. 1928] lxxi–lxxiii suggests that the eels may have been trapped in such land-locked lakes, producing perhaps a fat eel, unable to reproduce. The Strymon is a river in northern Greece. Whitehead [(1986) 71] notes: 'both sexes migrate into freshwater, where females predominate (the reverse in estuaries and lagoons).' The Greeks were not aware of the migration of eels to and from the Sargasso sea, though they knew something of migration and Aristotle believed they were born in mud, because of their apparent lack of sexual organs [*History of Animals* 569a]. Archestratus appears to refer to their having no organs. The interpretation of the Greek is here controversial: many editors, including Lloyd-Jones and Parsons (1983), understand 'having no backbone' or 'having very little bone'. We would argue that while 'having little bone' is possible, the eel is not unique in this. Nor of course is the eel unique in having no apparent genital organs, but this is a more striking aspect of the fish, and may have been prompted by the reference to pleasure in the previous clause. [On pleasure see Introduction. On the eel (*Anguilla anguilla* (L.)) see further Davidson (1981) 53, Palombi-Santarelli (1961) 198–9 and Thompson (1947) 58–61.]

FRAGMENT 9
[ATHENAEUS 285B]

Archestratus, the Daedalus of tasty dishes, says: Small fry [*aphue*]. Value as shit all small fry except the Athenian kind. I'm speaking of *gonos* which the Ionians call foam. Get it when fresh and caught in the beautiful bay of Phaleron, in its sacred arms. It is also of good quality in wave-girt Rhodes, if it is local fish. And if perhaps you desire to taste it, you should buy at the same time [sea] nettles,

nettles with long locks. Mix them together and bake them on a frying-pan, grinding the fragrant flowers of the greens in oil.

COMMENTARY

Context. 'The Daedalus of tasty dishes', is mocking, and implies excessive artifice: Daedalus is the mythical technician, among whose achievements were the labyrinth and the wings of Icarus [Apollodorus 3.15.8, Epitome 1.12–5). Recipes do not bear this out. 'Tasty dishes' (*opsa*) in Greek often means dishes based on expensive fish, inappropriate in this case. This introduction is found also in fragments 22, 25, 35, 57, 62; this type of preface is discussed in our own Introduction.

Content. 'Value as shit ...': this is surprisingly comic language. In writing about food, Archestratus has something in common with comedy, on which we comment in the Introduction. Here comic language (comedy speaks of shit with the word *minthos* either literally, or in a term of dismissal as here), contrasts sharply with the epic phraseology. Athenian small fry (sprats and other small fish of various species, equivalent probably to whitebait) are common elsewhere, and are one of those foods which Archestratus shares with comic commonplaces. Milesian sea bass is another. Sea nettles, or sea anemones, are combined with the small fry, and a dressing of nettles added (a linguistic joke in the Greek). The fragrant flowers of the greens may be the tips of the nettles which are to be eaten young, or other unspecified green plants to be added later. The eating of young nettles is mentioned at Aristophanes, *Knights* 422, other tender plants at Galen 6.635–6, 644 Kühn. Cooking in a 'frying-pan' (*teganon*) is common. Some of these have been found by American archaeologists in the Athenian *agora* [Sparkes (1962)].

Figure 9. A silver coin of Syracuse (c. 455 BC) showing a goddess and fish.

[45]

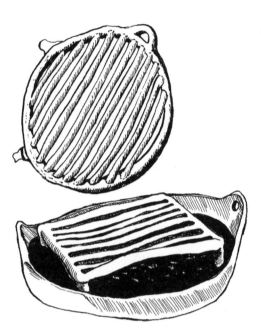

*Figure 10. Kitchen equipment: grills and a frying-pan (*teganon), *all in terracotta, found in the Athenian agora. The 'frying-pan' might also be used to hold hot charcoal under the grill.*

FRAGMENT 10
[ATHENAEUS 285D]

Clearchus the Peripatetic in his work on proverbs says, of small fry: 'because they need little heat in the pan, the school of Archestratus direct that small fry be tossed on to a hot pan and taken off sizzling.'

COMMENTARY

Context. This fragment comes from the same work of Clearchus, *On Proverbs*, as fragment 3. He refers to the school of Archestratus (literally 'those around Archestratus'), but the reference could be to cooks in general. The cooking of small fry is in a *teganon*, or frying-pan as in fragment 9, and as indeed in Davidson (1981) 44.

FRAGMENT 11
[ATHENAEUS 300D]

The *elops* must be eaten especially in famous Syracuse, for there you will find the very best. It originated from there in the first place. So when it is caught off the islands or off Asia indeed, or Crete, it comes thin and tough and battered by the waves.

COMMENTARY

Content. The *elops* is not certainly identified, but is sometimes identified with the sturgeon [Thompson (1947) 62–3, Apion in Athenaeus 294f]. It is also linked with other fish whose identity is uncertain, the *anthias* or 'beauty fish' [Dorion, *On Fishes* at Athenaeus 282c–d], and the *aulopias* of fragment 33. In this uncertainty, Archestratus probably does not have the sturgeon in mind [see fragments 21 and 23], though *Acipenser sturio* (L.) was the commonest of the sturgeons in the western Mediterranean [Davidson (1981) 38] and is known in Sicilian waters [Palombi and Santarelli (1961) 278]. The *elops* is, says Archestratus, one of those fish that suffers from travelling too far (compare tuna after spawning in fragment 34). He has travelling fish, fish in river, sea and lake, estuary fish, and so on: these are valuable categories both for the zoologist and the eater of fish. Our Introduction discusses Syracuse as a particularly favoured location in the history of Greek food.

FRAGMENT 12
[ATHENAEUS 328B]

Wise Archestratus in his counsels says The gilt-head [*chrusophrus*]. Do not pass by the fat gilt-head from Ephesus which the local people call *ioniscos* [little Ionian]. Get one of those babes of holy Selinus. Wash it properly then bake it and serve it whole, even if it is 10 cubits long.

COMMENTARY

Context. The introduction is probably sarcastic, wisdom and counsels being appropriate to more serious matters.

Content. The *chrusophrus* is the gilt-head bream [*Sparus aurata* (L.) in Davidson (1981) 75, compare Palombi and Santarelli (1961) 89], though see below. Note the mention of fat in the fish, a quality which we discuss in our Introduction. The ⁙⁙⁙⁙⁙⁙⁙⁙⁙⁙⁙⁙⁙ ⁙⁙ⁱes in the rich waters off Asia Minor. Archestratⁱ⁙⁙⁙⁙⁙⁙⁙⁙ ⁙⁙ local names or variants, here 'little Ionian', as is suitable in a work which covers many places. The practice is shared with writers of glossaries and related works, for example Dorion *On Fishes*, on whom Athenaeus often calls in his identification of fish names, as for example in fragment 14, and is similar to that adopted by Palombi and Santarelli (1961). Davidson (1981) follows a parallel course, though he is often recording names of fish in different languages. Hicesius comments on the excellence of the gilt-head [Athenaeus 328b] for sweetness and taste, as does Davidson. The fish was also sacred to Aphrodite. There is an epic flavour to the phrase 'babes of holy Selinus' (the river at Ephesus). This is a good example of a sea fish that is best in estuaries [see Thompson (1947) 292–4 on discussions in Aristotle and Pliny]. 10 cubits long for baking whole is an enormous size: over 300 cm, Davidson lists 60 cm as the maximum. Archestratus is making an absurd exaggeration (unless a different fish is at issue), though we should note that size was not as desirable as it was for the Romans [on which see fragment 14].

FRAGMENT 13
[ATHENAEUS 320B]

The parrotfish [*skaros*]. Bake the great parrotfish at Chalcedon by the sea after rinsing it well. You will also see a good and large one in Byzantium, carrying a body resembling a circling shield. Prepare it whole as follows: cover completely with cheese and oil and hang in a hot oven. Then bake well. Sprinkle with salt mixed with cumin and yellow-grey oil, pouring down from your hand the god-given stream.

COMMENTARY

Context. For the *Context* of this fragment, see the translation of fragment 41, below. Athenaeus says the *skaros* (almost certainly the parrotfish, *Euscarus cretensis* (L.)) is mentioned by Archestratus here and in another passage (fragment 41, which concentrates on the red mullet). If we assume that Athenaeus has not made a mistake, then Archestratus was prepared to describe a fish in more than one place: here the parrotfish of the Bosporus, in fragment 41 of Ephesus. Some scholars have doubted Athenaeus' testimony since Pliny

[*Natural Histories* 9.62] says that Cape Lectum in the Troad is the northern limit for the fish. Brandt changes the text of Archestratus so that a sea bream is referred to. Equally a different species of wrasse may be meant. We prefer to acknowledge an element of doubt and retain the parrotfish.

Content. Byzantium and Chalcedon face each other on the European and Asian sides of the Bosporus. Andrew Dalby (1994) believes, with the support of the majority of the best manuscripts, that the name Chalcedon is a mistake for Carthage. This raises more problems than it solves. The problem of distribution is not cured [see *Context*], as Byzantium remains, and another may be created; is Carthage beyond the presumed western range of the parrotfish? A further problem lies in Greeks being recommended to visit Carthage. Is this credible? Archestratus does not visit Carthaginian cities in Sicily, and Greek relations with Carthage were often very difficult; on the other hand, Greeks evidently did trade heavily with Carthage at various periods, and Dalby may be right. Non-Greek locations are discussed in the note on fragment 51 and in the Introduction. The method of suspending the fish in a hot oven rather than rolling in hot ashes or roasting on a tray or pan is similar to baking in that any fat drips away leaving the fish dry. This suits fatty items like lamb. The recipe counters any drying effect by packing on a cheese and oil crust. On reconstruction, the recipe works well, provided you are accustomed to the combination of cheese, oil and cumin. It is not a flavour combination that would suit more delicate fish. The parrotfish is a ruminant fish [Thompson (1947) 238–41]. Davidson [(1981) 109] is puzzled by its high esteem among Roman gourmets [Pliny 9.62 again]; this is not shared by Archestratus, who cheeses it and hangs it in the oven. There is an interesting note in Galen [6.718 Kühn] who says the parrotfish is best for pleasure: given that it is a 'rockfish' – a significant concession. It is likely that Roman interest was founded entirely upon the rarity of the fish in the western Mediterranean. Macrobius comments on this in his chapter on fish and gluttony [*Saturnalia* 3.16].

Figure 11. One in a series of fish plates (see figures 16 and 22, below) from Campania (the area to the north, south and east of Naples), some of which have a connection with a Sicilian school of painters. They are discussed by Trendall in Red-Figure Vases of Southern Italy and Sicily *(London 1989), page 162. In these instances, the dishes are often the work of known artists.*

FRAGMENT 14
[ATHENAEUS 316A]

Donkey-fish [*onos*]. And Anthedon nurtures a good-sized donkey-fish, which they call *kallarias*, but its flesh has a certain spongy quality and in other respects is unpleasant in my opinion. Others though praise it. Some of course like one thing, others another.

COMMENTARY

Content. The hake (*Merluccius merluccius* (L.)) may be meant, though of the *onos* Dorion [at Athenaeus 315f] says that it has many names. Archestratus gives an alternative name, just as he does for gilt-head in fragment 12. The listing of other names is reported in a quotation by Athenaeus [118c] of Dorion *On Fishes*, 'the so-called *mulloi* are called *agnotidia* by some people, and by others *platistakoi*, even though they are the same fish, as too is the *chellaries*. Now this one fish has received many names, and they also call it *bacchus*, *oniscus* and *chellaries.'* The *oniscus* may be *Gadus poutassou*, a smaller member of the cod family [see Davidson (1981) 60, Thompson (1947) 181 and Palombi and Santarelli (1961) 168–9]. Archestratus' *kallarias* is probably the same word as the *chellaries*, and is presumably the name used at Anthedon in Boeotia. Anthedon was a small fishing community on the coast of Boeotia opposite Euboea, possibly good for fish because in a channel with particular currents, and one of the more unusual of Archestratus' place names, the obverse of places like Miletus for sea bass and Syracuse for cheese that were clichés in comedy and food books. Members of the cod family are probably at issue here; the similar hake is identified as the best in the Mediterranean by Davidson [(1981) 64]. In specifying 'good-sized', Archestratus selects larger fish, as do chefs now. Small fish and giant fish are cheaper than optimum-size fish which tend to be fairly large. Very large means old. Archestratus describes the flesh as spongy; it is described among the 'soft-fleshed' fish in Galen [6.720 Kühn]. Archestratus acknowledges different opinions in others with 'some like this, others that': he is not as dogmatic as might be thought. Furthermore, he is prepared to consider fish that are not gourmet specialities, for example in fragments 9 and 40. Thompson (1947) [97 and 181–3] has more details. There is a gap in the text towards the end of the passage.

FRAGMENT 15

[ATHENAEUS 305E]

But if you go to the rich land of Ambracia and happen to see the boar-fish, buy it and don't leave it behind, even if it costs its weight in gold, for fear the dread wrath of the gods shall blast down upon you. For this fish is the flower of nectar. It is not allowed to all mortals to eat it or even to see it with their eyes: only to those who hold in their hands the plaited weave of the marsh-nurtured rope and are experienced in throwing pebbles in fiery competition and tossing in sheep bones.

COMMENTARY

Content. The boar-fish is a grunting fish of the river Achelous, according to Aristotle and Aelian. Archestratus places the fish at Ambracia, a town further west in Greece, on the river Aracthus, and mentioned several times by him. The reference to the 'rich land of Ambracia' is endorsed by the comment of Strabo [*Geography* 7.7.6], 'the city is remarkably prosperous'. [For the wealth of this part of north-west Greece, especially in fish, see N.G.L. Hammond, *Epirus* (Oxford 1967) 135–49. Dalby (1994) has further interesting observations.] Archestratus also mentions Ambracia in fragments 25, 30, 45, 54, 56. Aristotle [*History of Animals* 535b17] locates the boar-fish in the river Achelous some way to the south and east. Archestratus does not say whether the fish is a river fish or is caught in the gulf of Ambracia. Thompson [(1947) 101–2] believes there are two separate fish here. Archestratus' enthusiasm for the boar-fish is one version of a series of strategies, which includes stealing, also found in fragment 21. Equal enthusiasm may accompany the eating of the fish, as in fragment 22. Presumably in this case, divine wrath is thought to follow if the true worth of the boarfish is not appreciated. This divine interest in the food and comparison with nectar is found elsewhere, as we note on fragment 4. There is a comic fragment in which a speaker says 'this wine is nectar, and I must give it to all my friends to drink. My enemies will only get Peparethan.' 'Worth its weight in gold': Aristotle [at Athenaeus 305d] classifies the boar-fish as 'with very firm flesh', like the mullet or grey-fish or sea perch [so too Galen 6.727 Kühn], though the text is uncertain. He also says the fish is rough-skinned which may account for its name. The end of this fragment is unclear, both as to the reading of the text and the role of the throwing of the pebbles and the throwing of the sheep bones in catching this fish. Brandt suggests the following: the fishermen with their wicker baskets, unable to see the boar fish in the water, drop in pebbles coated in oil, in a circle. Visibility aided, and in addition enticing the fish with lamb bones, they can then pounce with their baskets.

FRAGMENT 16

[ATHENAEUS 312F]

And Archestratus the pleasure-philosopher says between ... and Italy in the strait with its narrow waves lives the moray eel [*muraina*] called the floater. If a fisherman catches one, buy it. It's an amazing food from there.

COMMENTARY

Context. Archestratus the philosopher of pleasure – virtually an oxymoron in Greek thought, as discussed in the Introduction.

Content. Another fragment in praise of eels, this time the *muraina*, the moray, *Muraina helena* (L.) [Davidson (1981) 54, and Palombi and Santarelli (1961) 202–3]. This is interesting because, despite an abundance of other fish, the eel is singled out for preference. The moray is as nourishing as the eel, according to Hicesius at Athenaeus 312c. [There is some confusion between the moray and the lamprey in ancient discussions of the *muraina*, as discussed by Thompson (1947) 162–5. Both are good to eat, as Davidson (1981) 54 and 25 explains.] The Sicilian moray, called a floater here, was later popular at Rome. Macrobius says [*Saturnalia* 3.15.7, trans. Davies] 'lampreys [read 'morays'] used to be brought to the fishponds at Rome from the Sicilian narrows, between Rhegium and Messina, for according to our spendthrift gluttons that is where the best are found, and indeed the best eels too. Both the lampreys [read 'morays'] and the eels that come from those parts are called "floaters" in Greek and Latin .... Many weighty authorities have made famous the lampreys [read 'morays'] of the Sicilian narrows ... Varro has said in his *Gallus or the Wonders of Nature*, "in Sicily too the *murainai* floaters can be caught by hand, for they float on the surface because they are so fat."'

Figure 12. An Apulian krater *(mixing bowl for wine) illustrating comic characters admiring a tray of foods while a slave hides a stolen item in his tunic. The vase is dated to the early fourth century BC. Note that the* krater *was the focus of the symposium and the object around which drinking and entertainment took place.*

FRAGMENT 17
[ATHENAEUS 322C]

But only seek a *sinodon* which is fat, and try to take it from the straits, my friend. I also, as it happens, say the same to you, Cleandros.

COMMENTARY

Content. Fragment 18 has a similar reference to fatness as a desirable quality. Most sweetness and flavour is in the fat of meat and it is only recently that lean meat has been perceived as desirable. Oiliness in fish has less widespread appeal now. Eels, herring and other oily fish have a more pronounced fishy flavour. If this is *Dentex dentex* (L.), Davidson [(1981) 78] pronounces it a fine fish. [See also Thompson (1947) 255, Palombi and Santarelli (1961) 87.] This fragment appears to be addressed to Archestratus' two recipients, Cleandros and Moschus. Moschus is mentioned in fragment 4 and by Athenaeus at 278e. The straits may again be the straits of Messina.

FRAGMENT 18
[ATHENAEUS 293F]

We must speak of the conger eel. Archestratus in his Gastronomy relates where each part of it ought to be purchased: The conger. You have the head of the conger, friend, in Sicyon, a fat and strong and large head, and all the belly parts. Then boil it for a long time in salt water, sprinkled with green herbs.

COMMENTARY

Context. Archestratus specifies different parts of the conger as good in different places. We cannot comment on this.

Content. The fat conger eels of Sicyon and the cooking of conger in salt water with green herbs for flavour are attested elsewhere. In comedy, one example of many quoted by Athenaeus [288c–294c] comes from Philemon's *The Soldier* [fragment 82 KA]: 'from Sicyon the beloved a conger, to be carried by Poseidon to the heavens for the gods'. The herbs here appear to be for flavour and are not acting as wrapping to protect the flesh of the fish from the heat, on which see fragment 35. The specification of head and belly is part of the interest in texture which is marked in Archestratus [Introduction, and in general, Thompson (1947) 49–50]. On *Conger conger* (L.) see Davidson [(1981) 55], and Palombi and Santarelli [(1961) 200].

FRAGMENT 19
[ATHENAEUS 294A]

Proceeding to the regions of Italy, this fine travel writer then says and a really impressive conger can be caught which is as superior to all others as is the fattest tuna to the worst crowfish.

COMMENTARY

Context. This is further sarcastic praise for Archestratus' thoroughness [see Introduction], adding the location. Since Archestratus is Sicilian, Italian details are to be expected, though Italians are criticized in fragments 45 and 62.

Content. Archestratus' enthusiasm for eels and similar fish recalls fragment 8. Again, texture must play a large part here, and fat, that being the quality

*Figure 13. A portable brazier for domestic use, found in the Athenian agora. A lidded casserole (*lopas*) is placed in position for a boiled or stewed dish.*

of the tuna specified. Tuna is found in fragments 34, 35, 37, 38. 'Crowfish' are considered by Thompson [(1947) 122–3]. These are perhaps not the Italian crowfish whose flesh is excellent according to Palombi and Santarelli [(1961) 46–51].

FRAGMENT 20
[ATHENAEUS 295C]
Archestratus praises the head of the grey-fish as follows But buy me the head of a grey-fish [*glaukos*] at Olynthus and Megara. For it is caught in the sacred shallows.

COMMENTARY
Content. The grey-fish is not certainly identified, as Thompson [(1947) 48] explains. Athenaeus [295b–297c] shows that its head was often sought after. Head meat is desired for its texture in countries such as China and Spain. We discuss this in Wilkins and Hill (1994a), and on fragment 18.

FRAGMENT 21
[ATHENAEUS 285E–286A]

Lynceus of Samos in his Letter to Diagoras *praises the small fry of Rhodes, and sets many Athenian products beside those from Rhodes: 'with small fry from Phaleron Rhodes matches the so-called Aenean small fry; with the sea lizard the* elops *and the sea perch. And her reply to sole from Eleusis and mackerel and any other fish they have is to bring forth the foxfish [thresher shark], a greater glory than all of Cecrops. The author of* Life of Luxury *advises anyone unable to buy the fish to get his desire by crime.' He means the chef Archestratus who in his famous poem says this about the foxfish:* In Rhodes the foxfish [alopex] is the dogfish [galeos]. And even if you risk your life, if they refuse to sell it to you, seize it. This is the fish they call fat dog in Syracuse. Afterwards, put up with whatever is fated for you.

[Athenaeus later [294e] quotes the same passage under *galeoi* (dogfish) in the following *Context.*] *Archestratus, who sought a life-style identical to Sardanapalus, speaking of the dogfish at Rhodes, considers it to be the same fish as the one carried round by the Romans with an accompaniment of pipes and garlands, and with the slave waiters also garlanded, namely the so-called* akkipesios [Latin *acipenser*].

COMMENTARY

Context. For the *elops* see fragment 11, for Sardanapalus the note on fragment 3, for the chef (*tenthes*), fragment 5.

Content. The 'Rhodian dogfish' may be one of the sturgeons, *Acipenseridae*, as distinct from other *galeoi*, the dogfish. Thompson [(1947) 42] accepts Athenaeus' identification. The Syracusan name, fat dog, however takes us back to the dogfish, and Thompson may be wrong to isolate the Rhodian from other dogfish. He thinks 'fat dog' may be an error for a form of sturgeon but this is worthless speculation. The desirability of a fish is considered in the commentary on fragment 15. Here efforts to acquire it extend to snatching and stealing, and paying for the consequences later. This, like the reference in fragment 9 to shit, is the closest Archestratus comes to elements of comedy: the stealing of food – specifically meat from a sacrificial altar – is a feature of the comic buffoon. Such stealing may also display failure to control sensual desire [Introduction]. Cecrops, an early Athenian king, here stands for Athens.

FRAGMENT 22
[ATHENAEUS 326F]

Archestratus the Daedalus of tasty dishes: In Aenus and the Pontus buy the sow-fish, which some mortals call the 'dug-out-from-sand'. Boil the head of this fish, adding no flavourings, but putting only in water and stirring often. Serve by it pounded hyssop, and if you want anything more, drip on it sharp vinegar. Then dip it well and hurry, even to the point of choking, to swallow it eagerly. The fin and the other parts of the fish are baked.

COMMENTARY

Context. As for fragment 9.

Content. The sow-fish, which Athenaeus [326e–f] suspects may be the same as the boar-fish, is attested in Sicily and here in the northern Aegean and Black Sea (Pontus) area. It is not easy to see the link with the boar-fish of fragment 15: Athenaeus is presumably judging only by the name. The alternative name suggests a flatfish. The head, cooked plain, is served with the pungent flavours of hyssop and vinegar. The former is comparatively rare in surviving culinary works. The division of head, fins and the rest (unspecified) again shows a concern for different textures. Greedy eating – to the point of choking – as in fragment 21 – raises a note of comedy, and perhaps gives some justification to the introductions to fragments 38, 44 and 54.

FRAGMENT 23
[ATHENAEUS 310A–E AND 163D]

*The dog-shark [*karcharia*]: concerning these fish Archestratus the Hesiod or Theognis of epicures says … Well, Archestratus in those fine Counsels advises:* In the city of Torone you must buy the underbelly of the dog-shark, the hollow[?] part below. Then sprinkle them with cumin and bake with a little salt. Add nothing else my dear except perhaps some yellow-grey oil. When it is baked, then add your pounded sauce and the trimmings. Now whenever you stew something [viz., fish?] within the sides of a hollow cooking pot, do not add water [text corrupt] or wine vinegar, but pour on it only oil and dried cumin together with fragrant leaves. Stew it over the heat of the charcoal without bringing it too close to the flames, and stir often in case it burns without your noticing. There are not many mortals who know of this divine food, nor do they desire to eat it, those that is who have the soul of a storm petrel or a locust, and are scared rigid because the

Figure 14. A late geometric krater *from the early Greek colony of Ischia (off Naples). Dated to the end of the eighth century BC, the vase depicts human beings being devoured by fish after shipwreck.*

creature is a man-eater. But every fish likes human flesh, whenever he can get it. So it's only right that all those who babble on in this way go over to vegetables and join Diodorus the philosopher and with him follow Pythagoras in a strict and severe fashion. [Athenaeus adds] *a part of this fish is what the Romans call* tursio, *the sweetest and most luxurious part.*

COMMENTARY

Context. The Introduction discusses the likening of Archestratus to Hesiod and Theognis. Theognis' name is given to a severe corpus of elegiac poems with moral themes, composed in the seventh–fifth centuries BC. The fragment is composed from two overlapping quotations in Athenaeus, the principal at 310a–e, the other at 162b–163d, which is a long passage on Archestratus' misuse of epic, Pythagoras [on whom see fragment 32] and pleasure.

Content. Torone is a city in northern Greece, in the Chalcidike. This fish is not certainly identified, but is probably a small shark, in Greek the sea dog. Small sharks and 'dogfish' are often merged in popular English usage

[Thompson (1947) 106–7, 1367, Davidson (1981) 28–31, Palombi and Santarelli (1961) 20440]. The underbelly of fish such as tuna was prized in antiquity, and Archestratus perhaps implies he is recommending a choice cut of something unusual ('not many mortals …'). This fish is not prized in Galen [6.728 Kühn] – 'its flesh is harsh and excrementitious and for this reason it is cut up and salted' – and it would be possible to reconcile the two by taking the underbelly to be the best part of the fish. The cooking instructions here are more detailed than often, the flavour similar to the recipe in fragment 13. Green leaves appear to be added for fragrance rather than covering, as in fragment 18. The slow cooking with herbs will work providing the cooking pot is covered, otherwise not. Fish cooked in this way is not easy to eat by hand as the stewed flesh is soft. It was presumably served with bread, perhaps in this case with a raised bread [see Introduction].

The later part of the fragment becomes philosophical, with comic elements. Attention is drawn to the mutual enmity based on eating between humans and wild animals and fish. The eating of flesh is part of an important debate in the ancient world, focussing on Pythagoras and the book of the neo-Platonist Porphyry, *On Abstaining from Meat*. The fear of being eaten at sea was also a popular theme, and appears on some vase paintings: for a discussion of human anxieties about fish and the sea see Purcell (1994). The debate is not seriously entered into here, but is conducted on the level of comic dismissal. On the eating of an animal before it eats you, compare Petronius *Satyricon* 66 (in the *Context* of eating bear's paw, which made the eater vomit): 'if a bear eats a man, how much the more should a man eat a bear'. A further comic element here is the newly minted adjective 'stormy-petrel-locustish' of the soul (note that it is far from certain that 'stormy petrel' is an identification of the *kephos*). Mention of the soul leads to Pythagoras' theory of the transmigration of souls and his followers' refusal to eat meat and fish because of their close relationship to humans and their possessing a soul. Diogenes Laertius in his life of Pythagoras [8.19] records, 'more than anything else he banned the eating of *eruthinos* [an unidentified red fish, perch or bream] and saddled bream and ordered followers to abstain from hearts and broad beans and, according to Aristotle, sometimes from sow's womb [on which see fragment 62] and red mullet.' This taboo is a regular butt of comic and other literature, some of which is collected at Athenaeus 160f–161d. One of the followers of Pythagoras, Diodorus of Aspendus, is brought in here as a

Figure 15. One of the fish plates of the fourth century BC from Cumae (see figure 5, above, and figure 20, below) apparently depicting, as often, some of the sea breams and another fish, here the torpedo.

ridiculous supporter of vegetarianism, and Athenaeus has other discussions of this philosopher at 163e–164a, immediately following our passage. Attacks on Pythagoras in poetry are of great antiquity: Xenophanes of Colophon (sixth/ fifth century) ridicules his theory of the transmigration of souls – in this case into a dog – in elegiac couplets [fragment 6]. Archestratus shares with other authors in identifying the vegetarianism of Pythagoras as comically austere, a form of exaggeration at the opposite pole to comic references to Epicurus as the purveyor of pleasure [Introduction, Athenaeus 101f–104c]. 'In strict and severe fashion' (*enkrateus*) alludes directly to *enkrateia*, 'self-mastery', the ability to control passion and appetite in the Greek moral system, on which see Foucault [(1985) 63–77]. The opposite of *enkrateia* is *akolosia*, 'lack of self-control', a vice attributed to the *kitharos* in fragment 31.

[61]

FRAGMENT 24
[ATHENAEUS 104F]

Archestratus in his much-feted poem: But leave aside a lot of the fancy nonsense and buy yourself a lobster [*astakos*] which has long and heavy hands but small feet, and advances only slowly over the land. They are most numerous and the best of all for quality in the Lipari islands. The Hellespont also gathers many together.

COMMENTARY

Context. 'In his much-feted poem' may be sarcastic or neutrally descriptive.

Content. Fancy nonsense, *leros*, is a comic phrase, for which compare fragment 35. Apart from giving a wide range for this lobster, *astakos* (whether spiny lobster, *Palinurus elephas* (Fabricius), or lobster, *Homarus gammarus* (L.), is not clear), Archestratus offers little, though he contributes to the finding of Thompson [(1947) 18] that they are rare in the Aegean [see also Davidson (1981) 178, 180]. The description of the lobster here is similar to the comic poet Epicharmus' description of the *karabos* [fragment 57]: 'there are *astakoi* and *kolubdainai* (crabs?) and the creature with small feet and long hands, the *karabos* by name'. There is much overlap between the species in ancient descriptions. The lobster's claws are here called hands, for which compare Aristotle's, 'they have claws not for movement, but instead of hands, for seizing and holding' [*Parts of Animals* 683b33].

FRAGMENT 25
[ATHENAEUS 105E]

Archestratus the Daedalus of tasty dishes advises: If you ever go to Iasus the city of the Carians you will get a good-sized prawn [*karis*], but it is rarely for sale, while in Macedonia and Ambracia there are a good many.

COMMENTARY

Context. 'The Daedalus of tasty dishes' is discussed at fragment 9.

Content. Fragment 56 has similar praise for the excellence of the Gulf of

Ambracia and the Macedonian coast for crustacea. Athenaeus [7b] remarks on the excellent prawns of Smyrna, up the Ionian coast from Iasus. There may be a pun between 'Carian' and '*karida*', prawn, which influenced Archestratus' choice of Ionian city: this however is contrary to his usual practice. Athenaeus records of the prawn [106d], 'Mnesitheus of Athens [a medical writer] in his book on foods says "*karaboi*, crabs, prawns and similar crustacea are all hard to digest, but are much more easily digested than all other fish. They should be baked rather than boiled."'

FRAGMENT 26

[ATHENAEUS 327D]

As Sirius rises [eat] ... the sea bream [*phagros*] .. in Delos and Eretria by the fair-harboured houses of the brine. Buy only the head with the tail to go with it. Don't bother to take home the rest [?].

COMMENTARY

Content. The text is missing or corrupt in places. This is one of the fragments with the season specified, discussed in the Introduction. Here Sirius is rising, in fragment 36 Orion is setting. The astronomical date varies slightly from year to year, more with latitude. The rising and setting of stars for the Greeks generally referred to the visible position of the star just before sunrise [M.L. West, *Hesiod. Works and Days* (Oxford 1978) 376–81]. Archestratus' model, Hesiod, used the same chronology. In the ancient world, Sirius rose in the latitude of Eretria on July 28th. For the importance of seasons compare Hippocrates *Regimen* I.ii where they affect the power or quality (*dunamis*) of the food. The species of sea bream is not known: Thompson [(1947) 274] improbably believes Archestratus is referring to an Egyptian species. The use of head and tail is surprising given the good eating quality of most of the sea breams (compare the probable gilt-head in fragment 12 and possible dentex in fragment 17). The eating of parts of the fish for texture and flavour is discussed in the Introduction. For the significance of the location of Eretria see the commentary on fragment 32.

FRAGMENT 27

[ATHENAEUS 30LC]

Archestratus, the company commander of banquets says: Get a *lebias*, the liver fish, in sea-washed Delos or Tenos.

COMMENTARY

Context. Athenaeus introduces Archestratus with a sarcastic military metaphor, an image common in texts on food, but very rare in Archestratus – his only reference to soldiers is at fragment 61. Matro employs the military imagery of Homer extensively [534.48–9]: 'forty black cooking pots followed him closely, but from Euboea an equal number of casseroles marched in serried ranks.' In this respect, Athenaeus is closer to the standard writer on food than is Archestratus. For the appropriateness of military images see our Introduction.

Content. The *lebias* is an otherwise unknown name for the liver fish, itself unidentified and linked with other unidentified fish [Thompson (1947) 146].

FRAGMENT 28

[ATHENAEUS 321E]

The *salpe* I always consider to be a poor fish. It is particularly to be eaten at the grain harvest. Get one in Mytilene.

COMMENTARY

Content. In general there is agreement with Archestratus that the *salpe* is a bad fish. This example may be *Sarpa salpa* (L.), described by Davidson [(1981) 88] and Palombi and Santarelli [(1961) 101–3]. As in fragments 9, 10, and 52, Archestratus includes inferior fish. The *salpe's* best time, here summer in Mytilene, is, according to the physician Diphilus of Siphnos, autumn in Egypt. The fish was known as both a shiteater, compare fragment 43, and a seaweed-eater (like the parrotfish of fragment 13). Davidson [(1981) 88] reports it is best in Tunisia during the vendange or grape harvest. [See also Thompson (1947) 224–5.]

FRAGMENT 29
[ATHENAEUS 320F]

The chef Archestratus in his golden words says: And in Thasos buy the scorpion fish, provided it is no larger than your forearm. Put forth your hands away from a large one.

COMMENTARY

Context. 'Chef' here is literally 'arranger of tasty foods (*opsa*)'.

Content. Here the scorpion fish is probably the *rascasse rouge, Scorpaena scrofa* (L.) [Davidson (1981) 147, Palombi and Santarelli (1961) 142–3]. Davidson recommends the cheeks: unfortunately Archestratus' opinions on the head do not survive. It is a firm-fleshed fish in Galen's category [6.726 Kühn], and according to Davidson it provides 'good helpings of remarkably firm white flesh'. It is unusual for Archestratus to deprecate a large specimen, though compare fragment 14. Davidson sets the maximum length at 55cm. [See Thompson (1947) 245–6.]

FRAGMENT 30
[ATHENAEUS 328A]

The *chromis* you will get in Pella – it's fat in summer-time and in Ambracia.

COMMENTARY

Content. The *chromis* is unidentified, but may be one of the *Sciaenidae*. Thompson [(1947) 291–2] believes it is the *Umbrina cirrosa* (L.) also known as *Sciaena cirrosa* [Davidson (1981) 99, Palombi and Santarelli (1961) 46–7]. It was identified in antiquity by its grunting noise and 'stone' in the ear [Aristotle, *History of Animals* 535b17, Davidson (1981) 96 and Thompson (1947) 292]. The *Sciaenidae* are valued now [Davidson (1981) 96–99]. The excellence of the *chromis* is attested by the early poet Ananius [on whom see Wilkins and Hill 1994b], quoted by Athenaeus [282b]: 'in spring the *chromis* is best, in winter the *anthias*'. [On the *anthias*, another unidentified fish, see fragments 11 and 33.] This fragment has three standard features: location (for Macedon and Ambracia recommended together, see fragments 25 and 54), fatness of the fish and season. Pella was connected to the sea (some 20 miles away) by a shallow lagoon, though Strabo [*Geography* 7 fragment 22] appears to speak of a navigable river. There is no apparent need in this case to consider a freshwater fish which perhaps grunts or has a stone in the ear.

FRAGMENT 31
[ATHENAEUS 306A]

Archestratus in Life of Luxury: Now the *kitharos*, provided it is white and firm [and large?], I order you to stew in clean salt water with a few green leaves. If it has a reddish/yellow appearance and is not too big, then you must bake it, having pricked its body with a straight and newly sharpened knife. And anoint it with plenty of cheese and oil, for it takes pleasure in big spenders and is unchecked in extravagance.

Figure 16. Another in the series of fish plates from Campania (see figure 11, above, and figure 22, below).

COMMENTARY

Content. The *kitharos* (i.e. lyrefish) is unidentified, possibly a flatfish [Thompson (1947) 114–5]. There are difficulties in identifying flatfish in Greek authors, exemplified by this and the next fragment. A possibility is the guitar fish, *Rhinobatus rhinobatus* (L.) [Davidson (1981) 34 and Palombi and Santarelli (1961) 243–4]. There are also textual uncertainties. The yellowish/reddish appearance is surprising to us. The larger fish is again valued, as in fragment 14, and cooked simply in (a light?) brine with herbs. The non-white and smaller fish is classified as lower in quality, requiring cheese and oil [compare fragment 45]. Details on cutting into the flesh in preparing the fish again indicate something more akin to a ray than a flatfish. A comic fragment has the *kitharos* baked [Athenaeus 306a–b]. The final line has a comic resonance: the fish enjoying the sight of big spenders and being unchecked in extravagance has acquired the characteristics of fashionable eaters who are criticized for eating fish, the principal gourmet food [see Davidson (1993)]. These big spenders however are eating the inferior version with the cheese dressing. The fish (whichever it is) is 'soft-fleshed' in the medical authors, inferior among the flatfish, and poor for eating.

FRAGMENT 32
[ATHENAEUS 288A AND 330A]

Archestratus, that Pythagorean when it comes to self-control says: Then get a large sole [*psetta*] and the rather rough ox-tongue, the latter is good in summer around Chalcis.

COMMENTARY

Context. Another sarcastic introduction. Archestratus is alleged to lack moral self-control [see Introduction]' and is said to be as abstemious in exercising that quality as Pythagoreans are with their food. 'Pythagorean' represents austerity and a diet without fish or meat, as discussed on fragment 23.

Content. There is some uncertainty about precisely which flatfish the *psetta* and ox-tongue are. In some texts they are identified as the same fish, in others distinguished, as here. In some medical texts they are characterized as 'soft-fleshed', in others as 'firm-fleshed'. The somewhat rough ox-tongue presumably refers to the skin, as in the boar-fish [fragment 15]. Size is again

[67]

Figure 17. A fifth century BC silver coin from Eretria showing a cuttlefish on the reverse and on the obverse a cow scratching itself, with a bird on its back. Eretria is on the island of Euboea, the name reflecting the quality of the land for cattle.

important [compare fragment 14]. Chalcis (if the reading is right), on the island of Euboea, is another site on a strait with unusual currents. Compare fragment 14 for the Euripus channel between Euboea and the mainland (also Eretria in fragment 26), and fragments 8, 16, 51, 56 for the straits of Messina. The most famous channel of all, and well represented in the fragments, especially for tuna [34, 35, 37], is the Hellespont and its chief port, Byzantium.

FRAGMENT 33
[ATHENAEUS 326B]

Buy the heads of the large young *aulopias* in summer when Phaethon steers his chariot in its furthest orbit. Serve it hot and quickly and a pounded sauce with it. As for the underbelly, take it and roast it on a spit.

COMMENTARY

Content. The *aulopias* is a kind of tuna according to Aelian, and is identified with the *anthias* by Aristotle [*History of Animals* 570b20, see also fragment 11, and Thompson (1947) 20–1]. The identification of the season by the mythical Phaethon is unusually ornate for Archestratus, but similar to fragments 35 and 36. Parodist though he is, he keeps such ornament under strict control. The *aulopias* is best in summer, which is also the time for spawning, according to Aristotle. For the head see Introduction; for the underbelly, fragments 23, 47; for the size of the fish, fragment 14. What exactly is meant by pounded sauce we do not know: presumably not the complex mixtures of Apicius, but herbs of some kind ground in a mortar.

FRAGMENT 34
[ATHENAEUS 30LF]

Now around holy Samos with its wide dancing places you will see the great tuna enthusiastically caught: they call it *orkus*, others call it the monster-fish. In summertime you must buy such cuts of the fish as are appropriate swiftly, with no fighting [?] over the price. It is good at Byzantium and Carystus; and in the famous island of Sicily the Cephalodian and the Tyndarian shores breed much better tuna than these. If you ever go to Hipponium in holy Italy, make your way to the garlands of the waters [?]: there are the very best [tuna] of all, by a long way, and they have the culmination of victory. The tuna in these waters are those that have wandered from there after travels over many seas through the briny deep. As a result we catch them when they are out of season.

COMMENTARY

Content. On the tuna, a migratory fish par excellence, see Davidson (1981) 125–6. In citing other names, as often [cf. fragment 12], Archestratus may refer to other members of the family, but probably gives alternatives for the largest tuna, *Thunnus thynnus* (L.), the bluefin. It should be bought in summer (if the text is correct), which is also the breeding and migrating season. There may be vigorous activity over the purchase [cf. fragment 15], but the text is uncertain. Archestratus attests to good fish in Samos, Byzantium, Carystus (the southernmost tip of Euboea), and even better in northern Sicily near Cephalodium and Tyndaris. In the modern world, Sicily is noted for its tuna fishing [see Davidson, and, for ancient versions of the famous tuna traps, Thompson (1947) 848]. Archestratus praises Hipponium on the Italian mainland as best for tuna, though there is uncertainty in the text over the meaning of 'the garlands of the waters'. Are they the shoals where they are caught? Notably, he says, the tuna in these waters have travelled far from there and are therefore caught out of season. It is difficult to see why, if he is writing from Gela in southern Sicily, the fish should be worse and further-travelled than those to the north of the island. This may conform to migratory patterns, with fish travelling westward along the north coast of Sicily and their breeding grounds and back eastwards along the south coast. We have not been able to verify this. There is a possibility that he is writing from somewhere else not blessed with tuna, such as Athens. 'With its wide dancing places' is a conventional epic epithet and may not convey anything particular about Samos.

FRAGMENT 35
[ATHENAEUS 278A]

Archestratus the Daedalus of tasty dishes in his Gastrology (for such is its title according to Lycophron in his books on comedy, just as the work of Cleostratus of Tenedos is titled Astrology) says this about the amia: The *Amia*. Prepare it by every method, in the autumn, when the Pleiad is sinking. Why recite it to you word for word, for you could not do it any harm even if you wished to? But if you desire to learn this too, my dear Moschus, the best way to present this fish I mean, then in fig leaves with not too much origano is the way. No cheese, no fancy nonsense. Simply place it with care in the fig leaves and tie them with rush-cord from above. Then put into hot ashes and use your intelligence to work out the time when it will be roasted: don't let it burn up. Let it come from lovely Byzantium if you wish to have the best, though you will get a good one if it is caught near here. The further from the Hellespont, the worse the fish: if you travel over the glorious salt ways of the Aegean sea, it is no longer the same fish at all; rather, it brings shame on my earlier praise.

COMMENTARY

Context. Archestratus is introduced again as the Daedalus of tasty dishes [see fragment 9]. Here also is a further comment on the title [discussed at fragment 1], interestingly by a scholar of the history of comedy, a genre some way from Archestratus' parody of epic, but related [see Introduction].

Content. The *amia* may be one of the bonitos [Thompson (1947) 13–14, Davidson (1981) 123, Palombi and Santarelli (1961) 10812]. The season is given, and an astronomical note added in the style of Hesiod [see Introduction]. In the fourth century BC the Pleiades set on April 6th. The *amia* is versatile, and a quality fish, hence cheese is discouraged, as discussed on fragment 45. The use of *leros*, fancy nonsense, is similar to fragment 24. In the cooking method described here, fig leaves impart a small amount of flavour, but their real function in this dish is to prevent the flesh from being scorched while cooking and to seal in any cooking juices. However, most cooking of this type in Archestratus is not in ashes. The advice on restraint in the use of origano implies the addition – automatically – of some herbs, in this and maybe all fish cookery. Herbs are not described in the poem as preserved nor as having any medical qualities. This may be because they were considered low-grade like vegetables. The *amia*, as the bonito now, is particularly found in the Black Sea and, says Davidson, travels south in the last three months of the year, which corresponds with Archestratus in date and in location at Byzantium and the Hellespont. As in fragment 35, the question arises of where *here* is. Is it Gela again? Crossing the Aegean for worse fish may imply east (from Athens) to Ionia, or south (from the Hellespont) towards Crete.

FRAGMENT 36
[ATHENAEUS 321C]

The wise Archestratus says: Whenever Orion is setting in the heavens and the mother of the wine-bearing grape clusters is casting away her long hair, then is the time to have a baked sargue sprinkled with cheese, a large one, piping hot, and cut with sharp vinegar – for its flesh is naturally tough. Remember to take care of every tough fish with this method. Now the good fish are naturally tender and have a fat flesh: simply sprinkle these lightly with salt and brush with oil for they possess in themselves the fullness of delight.

COMMENTARY

Context. As fragment 12.

Content. This is an important fragment, setting out the standard treatment of simple cooking with salt and oil for the flavour intrinsic in good fish, and strong additional flavours, usually cheese, for bad fish. We are surprised that a dash of vinegar is not prescribed also for good fish, to cut through the oil – the ancient equivalent of the citric tang of lemon. Davidson [(1981) 81] pronounces one of the sargues (*Diplodus sargus* (Linnaeaus)) excellent for eating, on which the doctors agree, as does Ennius in his Latin adaptation of Archestratus. Palombi and Santarelli [(1961) 76–81] confirm this estimate. Archestratus only agrees in the sense that the sargue is inferior in the first place. The season [compare fragments 26, 33, 35] is introduced in an ornate manner; the excellence of the sargue is not expressed, merely its timeliness. Orion set between April 28th and May 4th (depending on latitude) in the fourth century BC. Cheese and vinegar are prescribed for its tough/firm flesh [*skleros* is not a pejorative term in itself]. Size again is desirable, as in fragment 14. On the position of the sargue, we may perhaps compare the parrotfish [fragment 13]: excellent in its way.

FRAGMENT 37
[ATHENAEUS 303E]

Archestratus, that stickler for detail, says: take the tail of the female tuna – and I'm talking of the large female tuna whose mother city is Byzantium. Then slice it and bake all of it properly, simply sprinkling it lightly with salt and brushing with oil. Eat the slices hot, dipping them into a sharp brine. They are good if you want to eat them dry, like the immortal gods in form and stature. If you serve it sprinkled with vinegar, it will be ruined.

COMMENTARY

Context. Archestratus is called the *kimbix*, the penny pincher or miser. Here probably stickler for detail. In a book on fish and cooking no quality could be more desirable, in moderation. This introduction is one of those where Athenaeus has followed his philosophical models who declare detail, accuracy, care, all these good qualities, absurdly out of place in a food book [see Introduction].

Content. The praise of tail meat is unusual [see fragment 26 and Introduction]. Most gourmets find the tail drier and a little inferior to meat further along the body. This is indicated in the fragment: the fish is being cut into sections and not taken as a whole. The next stage will be salting down such sections [fragment 38]. As in fragment 36, vinegar is discouraged. 'Mother city' is a somewhat grand and comic phrase for a fish, though transfers of this kind from the human world are common in such writers on fish as Oppian [see Wilkins (1993)]. 'Like the immortal gods ...' appears to be simply a borrowing from the *Odyssey*.

FRAGMENT 38
[ATHENAEUS 116F]

Archestratus who sailed round the inhabited world for the sake of his belly and the parts beneath his belly says: [...] a slice of Sicilian tuna, cut at the time when it would be preserved in storage jars. The *saperdes*, that tasty Pontic fish, can go to hell I say, along with its supporters. Few there are who know it is a poor and feeble food. Take though a mackerel, three days out of the sea, before it goes into the salt solution and is newly introduced to the amphora – 'semi-salted', that is. But if you come to the holy city of famous Byzantium, eat again I beg you a slice of *horaion*, for it is good and tender. But the *gourmand* [tenthesl *Archestratus has omitted to list ...*

COMMENTARY

Context. The belittling of the travels and researches of Archestratus and the connection between food and sex are found also in fragments 1, 2, 3, 37, and discussed in the Introduction. At the end of the fragment the 'chef/ gourmand' [compare fragment 5] is censured for an omission, having been censured in fragment 37 for detail. (He is further censured at Athenaeus 11 7b for a trivial omission.)

Content. Note a further comic colloquialism in the imprecation against the *saperdes* (one of the small tunas or horse mackerels?: see Thompson [(1947) 226]). The fragment offers valuable detail on the salting of oily fish in *amphorae* for ease of transport, and on the different qualities, depending on the fish and the amount of time in the salt solution and whether the fish was in season or not (*horaion*). All of these considerations determined whether the salt fish was to be a cheap or luxury product. [On salt fish, and the pre-eminence of Byzantium, see Athenaeus 116a–122e, Braund (1994), Wilkins (1993).] The text is doubtful at 'poor and feeble food': Lloyd-Jones and Parsons (1983) read 'a poor fish and fine food', but such a sense is unlikely and not supported anywhere else. *Horaion*, best seasonal tuna, is discussed by Athenaeus at 116a–117c.

FRAGMENT 39

[ATHENAEUS 284E]

Let our fine Ulpian enquire why Archestratus in his fine counsels says of preserved fish in the Bosporus the whitest that set sail from the Bosporus; but let there be no addition of the hard flesh of the fish which grows in the Maeotic Lake, the fish which it is not lawful to mention in verse.

COMMENTARY

Content. Archestratus indulges in a rare literary trick, drawing attention to the fact that *antakaios*, the name for the sturgeon, will not fit into hexameter verse (though it will into comic iambics, and is named in comedies of the fourth century). Almost certainly a sturgeon is meant since the Maeotic Lake (Sea of Azov) is sturgeon territory. Furthermore, sturgeon was a quality ingredient in salt-fish processing: see Athenaeus 116a–c (quoting a sub-Hesiodic poem in the same genre as Archestratus). Whiteness in salt fish was prized.

FRAGMENT 40
[ATHENAEUS 314E]

Archestratus says but get a slice of sword fish when you come to Byzantium, the very joint of the tail. It is also good in the strait near the jutting headland of Pelorum. *Who is such a careful tactician or such a judge of tasty foods as this poet from Gela, or should I say Katagela?*

COMMENTARY

Context. The fragment is followed by a sneering remark based on comedy [on which see Introduction] and a military image [compare fragment 27]. The joke against Gela, which sounds like *katagelan*, 'to laugh derisively', is taken from Aristophanes, *Acharnians* 606.

Content. Archestratus is making no great claims for the sword fish in recommending a *slice of tail* [compare fragment 37, and, for the importance of texture, Introduction]. His work, for all its concentration on fish, does not dwell exclusively on gourmet foods; there is some consideration of the highly prized part of the diet of a wide cross-section of people [this is seen also in 9, 10, 14, 52]. Byzantium and Pelorum are at opposite ends of Archestratus' world (Pelorum is the promontory at the north-eastern tip of Sicily). Davidson [(1981) 131–2] remarks on the excellence of sword-fish steaks, especially around Sicily. [See also Thompson (1947) 178–80, Palombi and Santarelli (1961) 189–91.]

FRAGMENT 41
[ATHENAEUS 320A]

Archestratus in his Gastronomy The parrotfish [*skaros*] should be obtained from Ephesus. In winter eat a red mullet [*trigle*] caught in sandy Teichioussa a village of Miletus near the Carians with their crooked limbs.
[fragment 13 is quoted immediately afterwards with the introduction 'in another part of the poem he says ... ']

COMMENTARY

Content. The parrotfish and its preparation are considered in fragment 13. Ephesus is in the expected area for the parrotfish, as set out by Pliny. Athenaeus makes clear that the parrotfish was mentioned in more than one part of the poem: in other words, it is not merely a matter of a catalogue of fish each in turn. This passage is mainly devoted to the red mullet. For the seasonal note see Introduction. The liking of the mullet for the shore [seen also in fragment 42] is confirmed by Oppian [1.93–101]. The reference to Carians with their crooked limbs is a parody of the Homeric 'Carians and Paeonians with their crooked bows'. There are not many cases of such parodic word play in Archestratus.

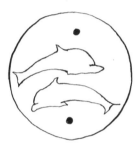

Figure 18. A silver obol of 550–460 BC from Thasos illustrating on the obverse two dolphins. Dolphins were frequently shown on the coins of a number of cities. As friends of humans, they were not eaten by Greeks, though they came across people who did eat them. Xenophon (Anabasis *5.4) describes the Mossynoeci who pickled sliced dolphin in amphorae and cooked with dolphin fat.*

FRAGMENT 42
[ATHENAEUS 325D]
The very knowledgable Archestratus praises the red mullets of Teichioussa in Miletus and then says And in Thasos too buy a red mullet [*trigle*] and you will get one no worse than a Teichioussa mullet. It is worse on Teos, though even that is good. At Erythrae they are good if hunted by the shore.

COMMENTARY

Context. 'Very knowledgeable' may contain a hint of sarcasm: see the Introduction.

Content. All four locations, Thasos, Teichioussa, Teos and Erythrae, appear to produce quality red mullet. The last three are in the southern half of the western coast of Asia Minor. The closest parallel in Archestratus for the grouping of locations that are near to each other is fragment 13, on Byzantium and Chalcedon. As in fragment 41, the shore at Erythrae is favoured for catching mullet. Both Thompson and Davidson comment on the great enthusiasm for the red mullet, especially in Roman authors, and Davidson notes 'the red mullets, especially [*Mullus surmuletus* (L.)], are among the most highly prized fish of the Mediterranean' [Thompson (1947) 264–8, Davidson (1981) 92–5]. Too little survives of Archestratus to allow any comment. [See also Palombi and Santarelli (1961) 32–5.]

FRAGMENT 43
[ATHENAEUS 307D]

The fine Archestratus says Grey mullet [*kestreus*]. Buy it from Aegina which the sea flows round, and you will share the company of smart men.

COMMENTARY

Content. One of the grey mullets [fragments 43–45]. The verb here, 'buy', is in the sense 'buy in the market'; in fragment 42 it is 'buy a desirable or tasty food product (likely to be fish)'. The distinction may be important, or may be poetic variation. Buying, shopping in the market, is a regular element in the foodlover's repertoire as recommended by Archestratus. Galen [6.710 Kühn] says that sea mullet are much better than river or lake mullet. They are herbivores [Aristotle, *History of Animals* 591a19–b4]; their scavenging makes them unsuitable for rivers polluted with sewage [so Galen]. Archestratus has no interest in river varieties, though Galen says the *kephalos*-type [fragment 45] swims in sea, lake and river, and Archestratus includes a lake *kephalos* in fragment 45. There is no immediate connection that we can see between Aegina and smart (lit. 'about-town') men. [See further Thompson (1947) 108–12, Davidson (1981) 140–4, and Oppian, who holds the fish in high regard (1.111, 4.127–46). Palombi and Santarelli (1961) 21–6 discuss *mugilidae* further.]

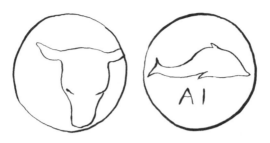

Figure 19. A bronze coin of the first half of the fourth century BC from Aegina showing a dolphin on the reverse, a bull's head on the obverse.

FRAGMENT 44
[ATHENAEUS 313F]

Archestratus the author of Life of Luxury: The grey mullet [*kestreus*] is amazing when winter comes.

[Compare Athenaeus 342d–e: *It is excessive gluttony to snatch food while still eating, and this particularly applies to the head of a grey mullet, unless those who are clever in this area know of something useful in a mullet's head! That is the sort of thing that the greediness of Archestratus could reveal to us.* And at 307b: *amazing are the mullets caught off Abdera, as Archestratus has said. Second are the mullets of Sinope.*]

COMMENTARY

Context. Athenaeus is quoting from Lynceus of Samos, *The Art of Marketing*, who says quotations of this kind from Archestratus may be used to beat down the fishmonger's prices if the fish is out of season. The grey mullets of Sinope are said by Galen to be excellent because of the rivers flowing into the Black Sea which create in their deltas lakes like the sea [6.711 Kühn]. Here, Athenaeus represents Archestratus as greedy and having an unhealthy interest in fish heads: these criticisms are clearly based on criteria other than taste, texture and nourishment, as discussed on fragments 2 and 3. On head meat see our Introduction, and on the importance of the season, fragment 26.

Content. Winter is the best time for grey mullet in Archestratus, autumn in the medical writer Xenocrates and in Aristotle [*History of Animals* 621b19–23].

FRAGMENT 45
[ATHENAEUS 311A]

The wise Archestratus: When you come to Miletus get from the Gaeson Marsh a *kephalos*-type grey mullet and a sea bass [*labrax*], one of the children of the gods. That is where they are best, such is the nature of the place. There are many other fatter ones, in famous Calydon, in wealth-bearing Ambracia and in Lake Bolbe, but they do not have the fragrant fat of the belly, or such pungent fat. The Milesian, my friend, are amazing in their excellence. Descale them and bake them well whole, until tender, in salt. When working on this delicacy do not let any Syracusan or Italian come near you, for they do not understand how to prepare good fish. They ruin them in a horrible way by 'cheesing' everything and sprinkling with a flow of vinegar and silphium pickle. When it comes to thrice-cursed rock fish they are the best of all at seeing to them intelligently, and they can bring clever ideas in a smart way to a banquet: little dishes which are cheap and sticky and based on nonsensical seasoning.

COMMENTARY

Content. Galen remarks [6.712–3 Kühn] that the sea *kephalos* type is best, 'the flesh being less fat and more pungent and sweeter'. The judgement is close to that of Archestratus, including consideration of the fat content and the quality of the fat. The Gaeson marsh was just north of Miletus and was joined to the sea. Galen recommends the lake variety (compare Lake Bolbe) for preserving with salt. The sea bass is similar, according to Galen [714], and inhabits estuaries and waters between salt and fresh, as here. The choice between simple cooking for good quality fish and sauces based on cheeses for lesser fish is set out also in fragment 36. It may be that Sicilians are mentioned here because they were particularly associated with cheese sauces, given the importance of the island in the cheese trade (such as it was: perhaps Sicilian cheeses had a status that led to a distribution wider than for other cheeses). Sea bass [*Dicentrarchus labrax* (L.)], whose Greek name, *labrax*, and Roman name, *lupus*, imply ferocity, is one of the most favoured fish for consumption [Davidson (1981) 67–8 ('an admirable fish'), Thompson (1947) 140–2, Palombi and Santarelli (1961) 44–5]. The Sicilians were associated with lavish dining, as we discuss in the Introduction. This reputation continued into the Roman period (see, for example Cicero, *Tusculan Disputations* 5). Cicero and his friends appeared to enjoy salt fish with a cheese sauce (*Letters to Atticus* 4.8; 14.16; *Ad Familiares* 9.16) – the status of the dish is not known. In attacking Syracusans and Italians, Archestratus appears to be advocating a style of cooking different from that prevailing at the time which was strong in flavour (cheese, vinegar, silphium) and expensive (silphium, a herb from Cyrene in N. Africa). Such a style is for rock fish like the parrotfish of fragment 13. Archestratus in this section treats other and/or earlier cooks to a mocking polemic similar to the one he himself receives from Athenaeus: their cooking is suitable for 'thrice-cursed' rock fish; they have smart ideas for the banquet [with an implication of little understanding?]; their dishes are cheap and ridiculous.

FRAGMENT 46
[ATHENAEUS 319D]

Selachians: now famous Miletus nurtures the best. But why talk of the file-fish or the broad-back ray? I would as soon dine on oven-baked crocodile in which the children of the Ionians take delight.

COMMENTARY

Content. The *selachi* are the cartilaginous or elasmobranch fish, the sharks and rays: rays are *selachi* in modern Greek. Thompson [(1947) 221–2] identifies the file-fish as the angel-fish, 'the most skate-like of the sharks' (when he says monkfish he does not mean what is meant in modern English, for which see fragment 47). This is probably *Squatina squatina* (L.) [Palombi and Santarelli (1961) 239]. It is of the order *Squaliformes*, the sharks and dogfish. [On sharks and dogfish see fragment 23, and see Davidson (1981) 32.] For the low estimation of rays compare Davidson [(1981) 33–36] and fragments 48–9. Where they are eaten, it is for the slightly gelatinous texture of the flesh, of which skate is the most prized example. The comment on the crocodile, probably the Ionian lizard of Herodotus [2.69.3], appears to be a further touch of comedy.

FRAGMENT 47
[ATHENAEUS 286D]

On the frog-fish the incredibly wise Archestratus advises as follows in his words of wisdom: The frog-fish. Whenever you see one, buy [...] and prepare the belly-section.

COMMENTARY

Context. Again, a touch of sarcasm is to be suspected.

Content. The frog-fish is almost certainly one of the monkfish or angler-fish [Thompson (1947) 28–9, Davidson (1981) 168, Palombi and Santarelli (1961) 187–8]. Compare the French name *crapaud de mer*. What here is called the belly section is the tail in modern English usage. The 'underbelly' is chosen also in fragments 23 and 33. The belly section of the frog-fish is included in a list of parts of fish for eating in the comic poet Antiphanes, fragment 130.5 KA, but otherwise excites little interest in antiquity as a food.

FRAGMENT 48
[ATHENAEUS 314D]

Archestratus says and an electric ray [*narke*] boiled in oil and wine, fragrant leaves and a little grating of cheese.

COMMENTARY

Content. The treatment seems almost standard – cheese, herbs, oil and wine – and is usually deprecated by Archestratus as in fragment 45. What is interesting is not so much that he uses it here with an inferior fish – this is perfectly rational – but that he chooses to discuss and advise on such inferior produce at all. The electric rays (*Torpedinidae*) are not rated as edible by Davidson [(1981) 33], though Palombi and Santarelli [(1961) 247–8] are a little less severe.

FRAGMENT 49
[ATHENAEUS 286D]

and eat a boiled ray [*batis*] in the season of mid-winter, and with it cheese and silphium. This is the method of preparation for any children of the deep which have a flesh that is not fatty. I now declare this for the second time.

COMMENTARY

Content. Dry, or at least not fatty, fish are recommended for treatment similar to the advice of fragment 13 for parrotfish and fragments 36 and 45. The assumption is that fatty fish are more sought after and therefore more expensive. It is strange to see the (presumably) expensive delicacy silphium used on them (see note on fragment 45).

FRAGMENT 50
[ATHENAEUS 304D]

The dolphin fish [*hippouros*] of Carystus is the best. As a general rule, Carystus is a place with excellent fish supplies.

COMMENTARY

Content. 'Dolphin fish', *Coryphaena hippurus* (L.) [Davidson (1981) 106–7 and Palombi and Santarelli (1961) 534], is not a certain identification: one of the breams is possible, as Thompson [(1947) 94–5] sets out. The dolphin fish remains more likely, for Athenaeus in the passage containing this fragment [304c–d] quotes direct identification by Dorion, *On Fishes* and Epaenetus in his *Cookery Book*. Davidson notes that it is 'good to eat and has a full flavour'. Carystus is in southern Euboea. The general praise of the sea off Carystus, which is in the form of a very large bay, can be set beside attestations for Anthedon, Eretria and Chalcis in the Euripus channel between Euboea and the mainland, as noted on fragment 32.

Figure 20. One in the fish plates of the fourth century BC from Cumae (see figures 5 and 15, above).

FRAGMENT 51
[ATHENAEUS 311E]

Archestratus says the latus *is best in Italy:* The *latus.* The straits of Scylla are home to the famous *latus* in much-wooded Italy, an amazing fish.

COMMENTARY

Content. The *latus* is the great Nile perch [see Athenaeus 311e–f, Thompson (1947) 144–6]. Thompson notes that Archestratus appears to describe a related but smaller fish in the straits of Messina, 'conjectured by some to be *Sciaena aquila* [the meagre]' [see Davidson (1981) 97)], which Palombi and Santarelli (1961) 48–9] declare to be a gourmet fish. This is a notable illustration of Archestratus' area of operation: the coasts of Italy, Sicily, Greece, the Aegean, the Black Sea. The Nile perch is the 'best of the Nile fish' [Thompson (1947) 145], but Egypt is not under consideration, and a lesser, Italian equivalent is preferred. (Compare the possibility of Carthage in fragment 13, which we also consider to be beyond Archestratus' area.) 'Much-wooded' appears to be ornamental, along with the straits of Scylla, a mythical reference (similar to that to Phaethon in fragment 33) for Messina. Nothing seems to be made of Scylla herself, whose diet combined fish and human flesh, a combination discussed on fragment 23.

FRAGMENT 52
[ATHENAEUS 313F]

Mormyrus. The inshore *mormyrus* is a bad fish and never good.

COMMENTARY

Context. The same as for fragment 44.

Content. It is not clear whether all *mormuroi* are bad, or merely the inshore variety. The fish is one of the breams, of less quality than the gilt-head or dentex (the likely fish in fragments 12 and 17). The medical author Hicesius judges them very nourishing [Athenaeus 313e]. This is probably a further example of Archestratus citing a fish that is not on the gourmet list. [See further Thompson (1947) 161.] The phrasing 'bad .. , and never good' is Hesiodic.

FRAGMENT 53
[ATHENAEUS 318F]

Octopus [*polupous*]. The best are in Thasos and Caria. Corfu also grows a great number, many of a good size .... octopus and dogfish

COMMENTARY

Content. For the octopus see Thompson [(1947) 204–8]. Other authors – such as Pliny, *Natural History* [9.91] – speak of their craftiness and liking for human flesh, a topic considered on fragment 23. Athenaeus [316a–318f] records much detail, including aphrodisiac and pleasurable qualities. Galen [6.736 Kühn] declares octopus, squid and cuttlefish nourishing provided they are boiled, but not always so. Thompson (1947) lists passages where octopus is tenderized by beating. Davidson [(1981) 208–16] discusses the cephalopods. (The gaps in the fragment indicate that 'octopus and dogfish' is quoted separately, albeit in the same passage.)

FRAGMENT 54
[ATHENAEUS 326D]

Archestratus who travelled round all lands and seas to satisfy his gluttony says Squids [*teuthides*] are to be found in Dium of Pieria by the surge of Baphyra. And in Ambracia you will see very many.

COMMENTARY

Context. Another version of fragment 2.

Content. Dium of Pieria is in southern Macedonia, north of Mount Olympus. Baphyra is the name of the Helicon river where it meets the sea. The combination of Macedonia and Ambracia is found also in fragment 30. Thompson (1947) discusses squid on pages 260–1; there is a comic recipe for squid stuffed with green leaves at Athenaeus 326d–e (immediately following our passage).

FRAGMENT 55
[ATHENAEUS 324B]

The greatest polymath Archestratus says cuttlefish [*sepiai*] in Abdera and also in mid-Maroneia.

COMMENTARY

Context. The allegedly misplaced scholarship of Archestratus is considered in our Introduction.

Content. In this fragment Archestratus mentions only cuttlefish from the Greek cities on the coast of Thrace. Details of stewed and roasted cuttlefish are given in Thompson [(1947) 231–3].

FRAGMENT 56
[ATHENAEUS 92D]

and Archestratus says in Gastronomy Mussels [*mus*]. Aenus produces large mussels, Abydus oysters [*ostreia*], Parium small cigales [*arktoi*], Mytilene scallops [*ktenes*]; Ambracia too supplies many and with them enormous [...], and in the narrow strait of Messina enormous *kongkai*, and in Ephesus you will get smooth clams [*leiai*] that are not at all bad. There are *tethea* at Chalcedon and 'heralds' – may Zeus destroy them, both the sea-born and the inhabitants of the assembly, one man excepted – that man is my comrade; he lives in Lesbos with its many grapes, and he is called Agathon.

COMMENTARY

Content. Aenus is on the coast of Thrace, Abydus and Parium on the Hellespont, Chalcedon on the Bosporus, Mytilene on Lesbos, Ambracia in Western Greece. Mussels were considered a cheap food [Thompson (1947) 166–7]. Ephesian mussels are remarked upon at Athenaeus 87c. Thompson [(1947) 190–2] has much on oysters as a food for the rich. We have translated *arktoi* as 'small cigales', but the identification is not certain [see Thompson (1947) 17–8]. On the scallop see Thompson [(1947) 133–4]. It is not known what is meant by *kongkai* [see Thompson (1947) 118], or by *leiai* (translated as 'smooth clams'), or by *tethea*. The 'herald' is 'a general term for a whelk', which has 'flesh [that] is tough' [Thompson (1947) 113–4]. Mention of heralds

Figure 21. Fragment of a fish plate from Gela (c. 350–340 BC) portraying an octopus with two other fish.

leads Archestratus into a pun with human heralds, dismissing them both as worthless. Denunciation of heralds is a regular feature in Greek tragedy; a more modern case is that of Montjoy in Shakespeare's *Henry V*. The warm tribute to Agathon is unparalleled in the fragments, the only men mentioned before being the addressees Moschus and Cleander.

FRAGMENT 57

[ATHENAEUS 399D]

On the hare, Archestratus, the Daedalus of tasty cooking, says as follows: The hare. There are many ways and many laws for the preparation of it. Now the best way is to bring the meat roasted to each guest during the drinking. It should be hot, simply sprinkled with salt, and taken from the spit while it is still a little undercooked. Do not let it distress you to see the divine *ichor* dripping from the meat, but eat it greedily. All other methods are mere sidelines to my mind, thick sauces poured over, cheese melted over, too much oil over – as if they were preparing a tasty dish of dogfish.

COMMENTARY

Context. See fragment 9.

Content. Here is a rare allusion to meat rather than fish. It is impossible to disagree with the cooking advice. The exhortation to leave the meat rare and make the most of the blood is also entirely consistent. Hare's blood is still considered a delicacy and is used to thicken jugged hare and most classic sauces for hare. The blood is traditionally kept thin by the addition of vinegar until needed and hares were sold with the paunch intact to preserve as much as possible. It is interesting that no provenance is given for meats and vegetables, but is for fish and breads. (Pretentious provenances are sometimes given in France to rabbit and other lesser foods.) *Ichor* perhaps recalls the juice that runs in the veins of gods instead of blood, implying that the juices are fit for divine consumption [compare fragment 4]. The term is however commonly used of bodily fluids including blood. The cheese sauce rejected in this passage is reminiscent of the fish cooking of fragment 45. It appears that the hare is to be served to overlap with the beginning of the symposium, or drinking session.

FRAGMENT 58
[ATHENAEUS 384B]

Archestratus in his much vaunted poem: feed up the young goose and prepare it also for simple roasting.

COMMENTARY

Content. 'Feed up the goose' does not necessarily signify forced feeding. This is a rare reference to poultry farming in Greece at this date. As for hare in fragment 57, the advice is to look after the ingredient rather than use involved sauces and garnishes. This attention to the quality of produce rather than artifice in cooking preparation is close to the modern approach. Buy the best and then, as Escoffier said, 'faites simple'.

FRAGMENTS 59–60
[ATHENAEUS 29B]

from Archestratus the writer on banquets then when you have drawn a full measure for Zeus the Saviour, you must drink an old wine with a really grey old head, its moist locks festooned with white flowers, born in Lesbos with the sea all around. I praise Bybline wine from Phoenicia, though it does not equal Lesbian. If you take a quick taste of it and are previously unacquainted, it will seem to you to be more fragrant than Lesbian, for this lasts for a very long time. When tasted though it is very inferior, and the Lesbian will take on a rank not like wine but like ambrosia. If some scoff at me, braggarts, purveyors of empty nonsense, saying that Phoenician has the sweetest nature of all, I pay no attention to them [... .] Thasos also produces a noble wine to drink, provided it is aged over many good seasons down the years. I know too of the shoots dripping with grape clusters in other cities. I could cite them, praise them, and indeed their names are well known to me. But the others are simply worthless beside the Lesbian wine. Some people of course like to praise products from their own locality.

COMMENTARY

Content. The advice on wine and the ironic comment that 'some people of course like to praise products from their own locality' show that the poem's advice is on the whole meal and its service, and that the strictures on gastronomy are directed at the host, and are not cookery hints for whoever

Figure 22. One in a series of fish plates (see figures 11 and 16, above) from Campania. Here, one of the fish is a cuttle.

is doing the actual work. Discussion of Greek wines is fraught. The best starting place is Lambert-Gócs (1990), who discusses ancient wines in the context of modern methods in Greece. In ancient sources for Greece, there is less systematic interest in grape varieties and vintages than there was in Rome at a later period. Archestratus' notes on Bybline wine appear sensible enough, but Athenaeus in a later passage [31a–b] clearly has no idea where the wine came from. It must also be said that there are no surprises in the locations selected, which is not the case with Archestratus' fish, though claims are made for many more cities. He is alert to vintages, though he refers to age with no precision. 'Braggarts, purveyors of empty nonsense' is a long, comically invented word similar to 'stormy-petrel or locust' in fragment 23. There is also much ornament in the language.

FRAGMENT 61
[ATHENAEUS 4D]

Archestratus from Syracuse or Gela says: All should dine at a single table set for an elegant meal. In all the diners should be three or four, and certainly no more than five. Otherwise it would be a tentful of soldiers, mercenaries and looters of foodstuffs.

COMMENTARY

Content. Diners reclined on couches, and generally had individual tables brought to them with the food ready served (this is certainly the case on vase paintings). Philoxenus of Leucas, a poet of the fourth century BC, begins his *Banquet* with tables being brought for several diners per table. One table for all seems unusual in the fourth century. For Rome, Macrobius [*Saturnalia* 1.7.12] quotes an authority as stipulating between three and nine diners. Archestratus comes within this band, though many Greek dining rooms had spaces for more than nine couches, as Athenaeus remarks [4e] when quoting this passage. This point is corroborated by archaeology. Mention of mercenaries as a disruptive force brings a very rare military note to the poem. Military language is not inappropriate to the kitchen, as pointed out in our Introduction and on fragment 27. The military imagery that pervades Matro has been discussed by Degani (1991). Archestratus may introduce mercenaries here because of their prominence in the wars of the fourth century [on which see our Introduction and McKechnie (1989) 79–100], or to make a clear contrast with the pleasures and decorum of the feast. The latter is likely, and is a similar feature to the exaggerated references to death at the end of fragment 62.

FRAGMENT 62
[ATHENAEUS 101B]

Archestratus the Daedalus of cooking speaks of sow's womb after the dinner and the toasts and the anointing with perfumes: always festoon the head with all kinds of garland at the feast, with whatever the fruitful floor of the earth brings into flower; dress your hair with fine distilled perfumes and all day long throw on the soft ashes myrrh and incense, the fragrant fruit of Syria. And while you are drinking, let these tasty dishes be brought to you: the belly and boiled womb

Figure 23. Part of a tomb painting from Paestum dated to 480–470 BC. The scenes portray men reclining at the symposium and enjoying wine, conversation, music and other entertainment. Here, the man in the centre flicks wine from his cup at a target in the popular game kottabos.

of a sow in cumin and sharp vinegar and silphium; the tender race of roasted birds, whatever may be in season. Have nothing to do with those Syracusans who drink only in the manner of frogs and eat nothing. No, do not be taken in by them, but eat the foods I set forth. All those other *tragemata* are a sign of wretched poverty, boiled chickpeas, broad beans, apples and dried figs. I do though applaud the flat-cake born in Athens. If you cannot get one there, go and get one elsewhere and seek out some Attic honey, for that is what makes it flaunt itself proudly. That is how a free man should live: the alternative is to go beneath the earth and the bottomless pit and Tartarus to destruction and be dug down countless stades deep.

COMMENTARY

Context. See also fragment 9. Athenaeus is concerned here with the place of sow's womb in the order of courses. Here Archestratus places it among the *tragemata* or tasty dishes at the end of the feast. These were as likely to be savoury as sweet.

Content. Garlands at the feast were obligatory: Athenaeus has a section on them [669c–686c], followed by a list of perfumes. There is a lavishness here in the celebration of garlands and incense on the fire, and also a secular form of celebration, mirroring the sacrifice where worshippers and animal wore garlands and incense was burned with parts of the animal for the gods. [On garlands in the Greek world see M. Blech, *Studien zum Kranz bei den Griechen* (1982).] The sweetness of sow's womb and fatty pork would balance well with vinegar. The dismissal of dried pulse and fruit is the only major lapse of taste by Archestratus. Their associations with poverty are irrelevant and there are many highly esteemed Mediterranean dishes – especially from the Middle East – which use them. This is also inconsistent with his suggestions regarding inferior fish [see fragments 9, 10, 49, 52]. Criticism of the Syracusans who drink without accompanying foods recalls their other failings mentioned in fragment 45. The recommendations for Athenian flatcakes are all the more meaningful because of the alternatives which use Attic honey. As with most of the advice there is a feeling of authority, of reading the words of someone who understands about food and who has spent time thinking about the subject. Archestratus may not be an experienced cook, but he is certainly a man who has eaten well and worked out for himself what was good or bad about the experience. Archestratus makes much of death as the unpalatable alternative to the life of feasting of the free man. Death is regularly regarded in gloomy terms in the straight epic of the *Iliad* and *Odyssey*; here there is a certain comic exaggeration to the theme. We might also note that death was a common theme in drinking songs and literature associated with the symposium. For example, Anacreon (a sixth-century lyric poet from Teos) reflects on old age, Tartarus and the journey to Hades while drinking [395 PMG]; Horace touches on similar themes in *Odes* [1.9]; Petronius' comic host Trimalchio has a strongly morbid streak in his *Satyricon*.

APPENDIX:
TWO RECIPES DERIVED FROM
ARCHESTRATUS

It is tantalizing to attempt some reconstruction of dishes from the past. The topic dealt with is still relevant: our daily intake of food, its flavour, as well as any nutritional content is of some interest to us all.

With Archestratus, two factors present obstacles. First, there are no recipes as such, merely allusion to what a dish may contain from someone who did not cook it. Often the advice will be more what to avoid – Italians with their greasy sauces, elaborate confections of cheese and pickle – than tips on how the dish should be either made or eaten. We are able therefore to establish a vague idea of the flavourings, perhaps oregano or fennel, but no notion of what quantity would be deemed suitable for an average-sized fish or sow's womb.

It is in fact possible to argue that this is no bad thing. Seasoning levels are partly a question of custom, and a trip into another era's judgement, were it to be truly authentic, may mask other more important facets of flavouring and cooking habits in the same way as any braised meat concoction from my mother's kitchen, or those of her generation, strikes me as too salty before it strikes me as anything else.

The second consideration covers the words we use and what may be actually meant by them. A dictionary may translate ingredients but cannot guarantee that strains of wheat or barley, grades of olive oil or vinegar, are the same as those implied by the same words today. In fact, it is unlikely that nothing should have evolved, either naturally or through intensive cultivation, over the past two thousand years. Only wild animals such as fish or hare are likely to be the same or similar.

This said, it would be absurdly academic to research a pursuit as functional as cookery without some practical demonstration of its results. Athenaeus' wanderings on the subjects of cakes and breads, even *kandaulos* – a Lydian speciality involving meat and cheese – provide enough detail for quite exact reconstruction. The fragments from Archestratus are less amenable, but these two instances have enough detail for some attempt at least.

There is another usable recipe involving boiled fish head that can be reasonably re-created if you are of a scientific rather than gastronomic disposition. The pounded hyssop that accompanies it was not to my taste and so, on the assumption that eating is meant to be a pleasure, I passed it by.

DOGFISH WITH CUMIN AND OREGANO
FOR 4 PEOPLE

4 x 150 g fillets of dogfish (smaller members of the shark family, called huss, rock salmon, rough hound, smooth hound, or spur dog, with long, almost eel-shaped bodies)
1 tablespoon ground cumin
1 teaspoon sea salt
2 tablespoons olive oil
1 tablespoon chopped oregano
outer leaves of a Webbs lettuce, wilted

Brush the fillets with olive oil and then season with sea salt and cumin.

Spread a tablespoon of chopped oregano on top and then sandwich the fillets together as if to re-form the original fish shape. You will then have two pieces.

Wrap the fish in lettuce leaves sprinkled with the remaining herb.

Brush the bottom of a heavy casserole with oil and place the fish inside. Cover tightly.

Bake in a hot oven until cooked: the time taken will vary according to the thickness of the fish.

Halve the fish pieces by either cutting each piece in two or separating the original fillets. Use any pan juices to moisten the fish.

MARINATED, THEN GRILLED, MACKEREL OR SMALL MEDITERRANEAN TUNA
FOR 4 PEOPLE

4 mackerel
200 ml nam pla
2 tablespoons olive oil

Nam pla is the Thai/Vietnamese commercial sauce made from fermented fish, salt and water, believed similar to the classical fish sauce, called *garum* [see Grocock & Grainger (2006)]. It is readily available from an Asian delicatessen or even a modern supermarket.

Prepare the fish by gutting and scaling it. If you prefer, the fish may be filleted.

Marinate the fish in *nam pla* for two hours, then lift out and pat dry. Brush with olive oil.

Grill and then serve moistened with a few drops of *nam pla* and a salad of bitter leaves.

Figure 24. Part of a banqueting scene painted on a krater, *a bowl for mixing wine and water, dating from the mid-fourth century* BC. *Servants bring foods to a figure reclining on a couch (not illustrated). That figure is dead: the couch is a bier. But the funeral feast is illustrated in a way closely related to the banquet for the living.*

BIBLIOGRAPHY

Arndt, Alice (1993) 'Silphium', *Spicing Up the Palate. Proceedings of the Oxford Symposium on Food and Cookery 1992* (Totnes).

Athenaeus, *Deipnosophistae* (trans. C.B. Gulick 1927–41), Cambridge, Mass.

Bilabel, F. (1922) 'Kochbücher', *Paulys Real-Encyclopädie der Classischen Altertumswissenschaft*, ed. G. Wissowa & W. Kroll II, 932–43.

Bini, G. (l965) *Catalogue of Names of Fishes, Molluscs and Crustaceans of Commercial Importance in the Mediterranean* (FAO).

Brandt, P. (1888) *Corpusculum Poesis Epicae Graecae Ludibundae* I (Leipzig).

Braund, D.C. (1994) 'Fish from the Black Sea: Classical Byzantium and the Greekness of Trade', in Wilkins, Harvey, Dobson (1994).

Dalby, A. (1993) 'Silphium and Asafoetida', *Spicing Up the Palate. Proceedings of the Oxford Symposium on Food and Cookery 1992* (Totnes).

Dalby, A. (1994) 'Archestratus where and when', in Wilkins, Harvey, Dobson (1994).

Davidson, A. (1981) *Mediterranean Seafood* (2nd revised edition London).

Davidson, J. (1993) 'Fish, Sex and Revolution', *Classical Quarterly* 43, 53–66.

Davidson, J. (1994) '*Opsophagia*: Revolutionary Eating at Athens', in Wilkins, Harvey & Dobson (1994).

Degani, E. (1990) 'On Greek Gastronomic Poetry I', *Alma Mater Studiorum* (Bologna) 51–63.

Degani, E. (1991) 'On Greek Gastronomic Poetry II', *Alma Mater Studiorum* (Bologna) 164–75.

Degani, E. (1994) = Degani (1991) in Wilkins, Harvey & Dobson (1994).

Foucault, M. (1985) *The History of Sexuality*, Volume 2, 'The Use of Pleasure' (New York).

Gowers, E. (1993) *The Loaded Table* (Oxford).

Gray, P. (1986) *Honey from a Weed* (London).

Lambert-Gócs, M. (1990) *The Wines of Greece* (London) .

Lissarrague, F. (1990) *The Aesthetics of the Greek Banquet* (New Jersey).

Lloyd-Jones, H. and Parsons, P. (1983) *Supplementum Hellenisticum* (Oxford).

McKechnie, P. (1989) *Outsiders in the Greek Cities in the Fourth Century BC* (London).

Palombi, A. and Santarelli, M. (1961) *Gli Animali Commestibili Dei Mari D'Italia* (2nd ed. Milan).

Parker, H.N. (1992) 'Love's Body Anatomized: The Ancient Erotic Handbooks and the Rhetoric of Sexuality', in *Pornography and Representation in Greece & Rome* (Oxford) 90–III.

Pearson, L. (1939) *Early Ionian Historians* (Oxford).

Purcell, N. (1994) 'Eating Fish: The Paradoxes of Seafood', in Wilkins, Harvey & Dobson (1994).

Rapp, A. (1955) 'The Father of Western Gastronomy', *Classical Journal* 51, 43–48.

Sparkes, B.A. (1962) 'The Greek Kitchen', *Journal of Hellenic Studies* 82, 121–37.

Thompson, D' Arcy W.A. (1947) *A Glossary of Greek Fishes* (Oxford).

So, Yan-Kit (1992) *Classic Food of China* (London).

Wellmann, M. (1896) 'Archestratus', *Paulys Real Encyclopadie der Classischen Altertums-wissenschaft*, ed. G. Wissowa 2, 459–60.

Whitehead, PJ.P. *et al.* (1986) *Fishes of the North-eastern Atlantic and the Mediterranean* (Unesco, Paris).

Wilkins, J.M. (1992) 'Public (and Private) Dining in Ancient Greece 450–300 BC', *Public Eating. Oxford Symposium on Food and Cookery 1991* (London) 306–10.

Wilkins, J.M. (1993) 'Social Status and Fish in Greece and Rome', in G. & V. Mars, *Food, Culture and History* (London).

Wilkins, J.M., Harvey, E.D., Dobson, M. (eds.) (1994) *Food in Antiquity* (Exeter).

Wilkins, J.M. (1994) 'A Taste for the Unacceptable', *Omnibus* (forthcoming).

Wilkins, J.M. and Hill, S. (1993) 'The Flavours of Ancient Greece', in *Spicing Up the Palate, Proceedings of the Oxford Symposium on Food and Cookery 1992* (Totnes) .

Wilkins, J.M. and Hill, S. (1994a) 'Fishheads of Ancient Greece', in *Look and Feel. Proceedings of the Oxford Symposium on Food and Cookery 1993* (Totnes).

Wilkins, J.M. and Hill, S. (1994b) 'The Sources and Sauces of Athenaeus', in Wilkins, Harvey & Dobson (1994).

BIBLIOGRAPHY FOR THE SECOND EDITION

Braund, D. and Wilkins, J. (eds) (2000) *Athenaeus and his World* (Exeter).

Dalby, A. (1996) *Siren Feasts* (London).

Dalby, A. (2000) *Empire of Pleasures* (London).

Dalby, A. (2003) *Food in the Ancient World from A to Z* (London).

Detienne, M. (1977) *Les Jardins d'Adonis* (Paris), translated as *The Gardens of Adonis* (Princeton 1994).

Detienne, M. and Vernant, J-P. (1979) *La Cuisine du Sacrifice* (Paris), translated as *The Cuisine of Sacrifice* (Chicago 1989).

Donahue, J. (2005) *The Roman Community at Table during the Principate* (Ann Arbor).

Dunbabin, K.M. (2003) *The Roman Banquet: Images of Conviviality* (Cambridge).

Garnsey, P.D.A. (1988) *Famine and Food Supply in the Graeco-Roman World* (Cambridge).

Garnsey, P.D.A. (1999) *Food and Society in Classical Antiquity* (Cambridge).

Grocock, C. and Grainger, S. (2006) *Apicius* (Totnes).

Grant, M. (2000) *Galen On Food and Diet* (London).

Hordern, P. and Purcell, N. (2000) *The Corrupting Sea* (Oxford).

Jacob, C. (2000) 'Athenaeus the Librarian', in Braund and Wilkins 2000: 85–110.

Jacob, C. (2001) 'Ateneo, o il Dedalo delle Parole', in L. Canfora (ed) *Ateneo: I Deipnosofisti* (Rome) xi–cxvi.

Lenfant, D. (ed.) (2007) *Athénée et les Fragments d'Historiens* (Paris) .

Longo, O. and Scarpi, P. (eds) (1989) *Homo Edens* (Verona).

Murray, O. (ed.) (1990) *Sympotica* (Oxford).

Murray, O. and Tecusan, M. (eds) (1995) *In Vino Veritas* (London).

Olson, S.D. and Sens, A. (2000) *Archestratos of Gela: Greek Culture and Cuisine in the Fourth Century BC* (Oxford).

Powell, O. (2003) *Galen: On the Properties of Foodstuffs* (Cambridge).

Rodinson, M., Arberry, A. and Perry, C.(2001) *Medieval Arab Cookery* (Totnes).

Roller, M. (2006) *Dining Posture in Ancient Rome* (Princeton).

Sallares, R. (1991) *The Ecology of the Ancient Greek World* (London).

Schmitt-Pantel, P. (1992) *La Cité au Banquet* (Paris).

Scully, T. (1995) *The Art of Cookery in the Middle Ages* (Woodbridge).

Slater, W. (ed.) (1991) *Dining in a Classical Context* (Ann Arbor).

Vössing, K. (2004) *Mensa Regia: Das Bankett bein hellenistischen Konig und beim Romischen Kaiser* (Munich & Leipzig).

Wilkins, J. (2000) *The Boastful Chef* (Oxford).

Wilkins, J. (2007) 'Vers une histoire sympotique', in Lenfant 2007: 29–39.

Wilkins, J. (2008) 'Athenaeus the Navigator', in *Journal of Hellenic Studies* 128: 132–52.

Wilkins, J. and Hill, S. (1995) 'Mithaikos and other Greek Cooks', in H. Walker (ed.) *Cooks and Other People. Proceedings of the Oxford Food Symposium 1995* (Totnes).

Wilkins, J. and Hill, S. (2006) *Food in the Ancient World* (Oxford).

Wilkins, J., Harvey, D. and Dobson, M. (eds) (1995) *Food in Antiquity* (Exeter).

Zecchini, G. (1989) *La Culture Storica di Ateneo* (Milan).

INDEX

This is an index, by page number, to names of people, places, books and fish. It excludes most of the other ingredients referred to in the text, and does not treat references to modern authors and authorities. However, classical authors cited in both text and commentary, except Archestratus and Athenaeus, are indexed.